My Path is Jesus

RICKY CLEMONS

PUBLISHED BY FIEDLI PUBLISHING, INC.

Copyright ©2019, Ricky Clemons

ALL RIGHTS RESERVED.

No part of this publication may be reproduced, stored in a retrieval system, or transmitted in any form or by any means—electronic, mechanical, photo-copy, recording, or any other—except for brief quotation in reviews, without the prior permission of the author or publisher.

ISBN: 978-1-948638-67-8

Published by

Fideli Publishing, Inc.
119 W. Morgan St.
Martinsville, IN 46151
www.FideliPublishing.com

Table of Contents

Spiritual Medicine 2
Don't Care About… 3
Let the Holy Spirit 4
A Natural Thing 5
Life Can Take Us 6
You Didn't Walk By Me 7
Live For 8
Can't Compare Jesus 9
We Can't Judge the Truth 10
Our Hereditary Tendencies 11
For as Long as You Live 12
Getting More and More 13
God's Love 14
Just By 15
There is No Jealousy in Love 16
No One but Jesus is Perfect 17
The Lord Has Given 18
If You Don't Have Jesus 19
There are People 20
You Watched Over Me 21
Jesus Will Always See 22
Love Is 23
Your Human Rights 24
I Didn't Grow Up Knowing a Lot of Truth 25

Jesus Wants Our Prayers from Our Hearts..................................26
If Life was Always Easy to Live 27
Not Wise..28
God Doesn't Control Anyone 29
On Mere Human Intelligence 30
Our Faith in Jesus Christ 31
Beyond All 32
Being Wise 33
Memories..34
If We 35
God's Ways 36
The Lord is Always on Time 37
It's Never Good 38
So Smart 39
By the Choices You Make 40
So Poor When It Comes to Spiritual Things..................41
Means Something...42
I Would be a Fool to Keep My Eyes on People 43
It's Nothing New Today 44
O Lord, You Always Know 45
Changeable Ways 46
We Must Look at Jesus 47
Proud People...48
The Best Kind of People..49
The Slavery that Gives Us Freedom 50

The Answer	51
We Can't Leave Jesus Out of Life	52
So Unexpected	53
Can Use You	54
Under the Sun, Moon and Stars	55
If Jesus is Not in It	56
Why Should You Worship?	57
It's Hard	58
Our Faith in the Lord is Being Tested	59
It's Not the Quantity, It's the Quality	60
You Can't Please Everybody	61
I Don't Want to Believe	62
Love is Freedom	63
Go Back in the Past	64
Jesus' Holy Name	65
Only for a Short Time	66
Created in the Image of God	67
When I was a Little Child	68
It's Wrong to be Thinking About	69
It's Sin that Comes Out of the Closet	70
Being Talked About	71
Many People	72
In the Shed of Our Hearts	73
It's Not So Easy	74
If We Love	75

Who Can Suffer More than God?	76
Many People Will Judge Me	77
Up in High Places	78
Where is God?	79
Why Me?	80
Jesus Can Give Us the Strength	81
We Can Tailgate Our Own Life	82
Pleasing You, My Lord	83
We Can Come So Close	84
From You, O Lord	85
On This Day in Time	86
We Can Ill Life	87
Wherever I Go	88
Life is a Pathway	89
The Best People to Be Around	90
Grief Over a Loved One	91
A Ram in the Bush	92
When There is Nothing Left	93
When I Don't See My Way Through	94
Blow Our Minds	95
Heaven is So High	96
Are Actions Always True?	97
When Has Love Ever Hurt Anyone?	98

Will Put Their Trust In 99
Today 100
Some Questions Will Never be Answered 101
Nobody Can Take Away 102
Life Can Make Us or Break Us 103
We Were Born to Serve 104
Rotating on Its Axis 105
Everybody in Church 106
Love to Talk About 107
The Beginning 108
The Path of the World 109
Only Imaginary 110
If We Question the Lord 111
Life is Full 112
Our Prayer Guard 113
God is Ongoing and Non-Stop 114
The Last 115
I Can Always be Myself 116
Cover Up 117
It Was My Cross 118
What Does it Add Up To? 119
In Simple Ways 120
We Can Live in Fantasy in the Church 121
A Dream to Hold Onto 122
The Greatest 123

Will Sooner or Later
Show and Tell 124
To Live Another Day 125
If We are Christians 126
Are We Ready 127
Will Never be Satisfied with Anything 128
Pain Can Make Us Stronger 129
Not Keeping Watch 130
Is Not Alone 131
Many People in Church... 132
It Would Be Great to See 133
God Made Things 134
If It's Not One Thing,
It's Another... 135
It Would be Wrong.. 136
We Will Never Run Out of Needs 137
Like a Mystery 138
The Heart Will Speak Actions.................................... 139
Make a Spiritual Investment 140
Living a Mountain Life 141
Doing Right by You, O Lord...................................... 142
Don't Always Have to Let Others Know 143
Strange Things Are Happening.................................. 144
Will Not Last Forever.. 145
Nobody is Left Out.. 146
We Can Always be Sure 147

Jesus Came From Eternity	148
Jesus Cares About	149
I Can Call You Up	150
I Would Rather Be	151
The Light Within Me	152
I Will Live Again	153
As I Get Older	154
The Lord Will Do Us Good	155
I May Not	156
The True Joy About Life	157
Wherever Life Takes Me	158
A Day Can Make Us Feel	159
What We Believe	160
What Can We Call Our Own?	161
You Keep a Record	162
Only One True Living God	163
I am a Pilgrim	164
A Sincere Prayer	165
Which Direction Will We Go?	166
Some Things We Must Leave Alone	167
My Life Is Not About Me	168
If We Hold Onto Jesus	169
Number One	170
Do Good Things in Jesus' Name	171
Our Name is Precious to Jesus	172
There is Nothing You Can't Do	173

Help Me to Represent You 174
You, O Lord, Gave Me 175
The Most Beautiful House 176
Jesus is the Living, Open Door 177
The Bridge of Eternity 178
Beyond Science 179
It Blows My Mind 180
In Church 181
It's the Holy Spirit 182
The Best Way 183
If I Was Rich 184
Real Life Can Be Complicated 185
The Kind of World We Live In 186
We Are 187
Who's to Say? 188
Only About This Life 189
Just Because 190
We Must Keep Ourselves Busy for the Lord 191
The After Life 192
We Don't Know What We Are Made Of 193
We Say We Are Christians 194
Time Needs a Promotion 195
If the Lord Is Not In 196
Compared to the Eternal Life 197
Sickness and Death 198
It Takes a Lot to Live 199

To be a God	200
Do We Ever?	201
As Long as I Do Your Will	202
So Amazing	203
You and I Can Choose	204
The Lord Can Give Us the Strength	205
The Sound of Life	206
A Spiritual Good Flavor	207
To a Desolate Place	208
Won't Control Us	209
We Exist	210
A Love Letter to Life	211
You Are Not Finished with Me Yet	212
Real, True Living	213
There is an Eternal Place	214
But What About in Between	215
Way Beyond Dreams in the Night	216
God's Eyes	217
Eternity is All Present	218
Shake Your Head at Me	219
Will Show Something	220
Divine Moment	221
Real	222
There is No Love in Being Selfish	223
The Lord's Green Light of Truth	224
Below the Sky	225

Some who know me..226

Leaning to the Ways of Babylon 227

Promise 228

You Were Always There for Me 229

Jesus will not stop blessing you 230

Us All...231

Ways 232

Pure and Innocent..233

I am Not Worthy..234

Jesus Christ was a Carpenter 235

Our Souls..236

Fathers Who Love Their Children..237

In Real Life 238

Will Give...239

God, Himself, Gave...240

Ancient Women of Greatness 241

Can Carry 242

We Know 243

Are We Like 244

The Righteousness of Jesus 245

In the School of Life 246

It's a Very Thin Line...247

We Must Love One Another 248

No One Can Question Jesus About Me 249

If You Don't Love Jesus 250

Our choices	251
We Are All No Good	252
We Will Forever Be Learning	253
In the Belly of the Whale	254
Feelings	255
Good Health	256
Everybody in the Church	257
Keep Your Eyes on Jesus	258
Can Say	259
Walking Through the Door of Life	260
We Don't Know Life	261
Chances	262
Doesn't Make You Better	263
No Comparison	264
Will Outweigh	265
Growing Up in the Lord	266
Will Give Luck the Glory	267
Change	268
Love Can Surely Get Our Attention	269
The Good You Put Off Today	270
We Don't Always Trust the Lord	271
The Lord's Tests	272
God Created Man and Woman	273
Will Always Look Out for Us	274
Disguise	275

Having Faith in Jesus 276
When Jesus comes back again 277
Shouldn't Take for Granted 278
Give Jesus some of your time 279
Can Only Do What God Allows 280
Doesn't Get People's Attention 281
In This World 282
No One Will Ever 283

My Path is Jesus

My path is my Lord and savior Jesus Christ.

The path I want to walk on for the rest of my life.

O, what a narrow path I can always trust to walk on because Jesus, my Lord, is a lot more than just talk.

The Holy Spirit loves to take me up and down my path that will always lead me to God's holy ground.

Jesus is my path to lead me to His house of salvation that I can rest in and know God's love.

Straight and narrow is the way in my path each and every day.

Jesus is who I can always trust beyond words to say.

There will never be any bushes and weeds growing in my path that is Jesus.

He will supply all of my needs.

The paths in this world can have snakes and wild beasts on them and they can be dangerous.

Jesus is my path to never cease to be safe to walk on and through with a peace that calms the storms.

Spiritual Medicine

Good medicine can heal a mental illness but it can't get the sin out of the mind.

Good medicine can heal a physical illness but it can't get the sin out of the flesh.

Good medicine is from the Lord Jesus Christ, who will heal our broken lives if we confess and repent of all our sins unto him.

Jesus is the only one who can cleanse us of our sins.

Jesus loves to give us good spiritual medicine from His holy word of truth.

The truth can set us free from the bad, sinful medicine that makes us sick in sin.

Jesus has spiritual medicine that's always good for our souls and lets us be healed in Jesus with newness of life.

Good medicine can heal the brain and body and make it function normally, but it can't rid us of our sins in our thoughts and in our flesh.

Don't Care About...

Alcohol don't care about who you are.

They can bring you down to nothing under all the stars.

Cigarettes don't care about who you are.

They can ruin your health no matter if you have a good heart.

Drugs don't care about who you are.

They can ruin your life and you'll have to pay a heavy price.

Crimes don't care about who you are.

They can violently attack you and kill you and your life will be through.

Sin don't care about who you are.

Sin will cause your soul to be lost and you won't walk on those streets made of pure gold.

Love don't care about who you are.

Love will love you because love is God, who is the highest love to have.

He will bring you and me to eternal heaven.

Death don't care about who you are.

It will write your name on the grave whether you're saved or not saved in Jesus who has no blame.

Let the Holy Spirit

Some people will mean you good and well, but you must let the Holy Spirit lead you to show and tell to see the outcome of things.

People can cause you to say the wrong words but the Holy Spirit will give you the right words, day after day.

People can cause you to do the wrong things but the Holy Spirit will cause you to do the right thing to mean something good.

You must let the Holy Spirit lead you and guide you with everything you say and everything you do and you will never go wrong.

Jesus Christ was filled with the Holy Spirit every day that he lived on earth among many stiff-necked people who were so against him.

Jesus never said anything wrong and He never did anything wrong because He was always strong in the Holy Spirit.

People can get you off the right track. Let the Holy Spirit guide you back to the Lord who you and I can't afford to stay away from.

Some people will say that they have the Holy Spirit and will gun you down with their words if you disagree with them.

Without the Holy Spirit living in you and me, we would be like broken limbs on a tree that can't even hold up the birds.

A Natural Thing

It's a natural thing to listen to your conscious.

It's a natural thing for a man to fall in love with a woman.

It's a natural thing for a woman to love a man.

It's a natural thing for a man to work.

It's a natural thing for a woman to give birth.

It's a natural thing to eat food.

It's a natural thing to drink water.

It's a natural thing to get some sleep.

It's a natural thing to tell the truth.

It's a natural thing to have good hygiene.

It's a natural thing to love.

It's a natural thing for a man to marry a woman.

It's a natural thing for a woman to marry a man.

It's a natural thing to believe in Jesus Christ.

It's a natural thing to worship Jesus Christ.

It's a natural thing to obey Jesus Christ.

It's a natural thing for the truth to set us free from lies.

It's a natural thing to wait on the Lord Jesus Christ.

Life Can Take Us

Life can take us under some tunnels of time that are not always on our side under the sun that shines.

Life can take us across the bridge of hope that we can have in Jesus Christ who can help us to cope with any problem that comes our way.

Life can take us on the highways of grieving over loved ones who are gone to the dust of the earth.

Life can take us down the country roads of having peace of mind that Jesus gives to us to know that he is for us wherever we go.

Life can take us on the ocean waters of putting our trust in Jesus each and every day. He is our best friend till the end of our voyage in life.

Life can take us on the beach of experience that we need to teach ourselves to hold on to Jesus who is more present than the strong winds that can blow the sand all over us.

Life can take us wherever Jesus Christ wants us to go in this life.

You Didn't Walk By Me

You were there with me, O Lord, in all of my yesterdays and you didn't walk by me and let me die in my sinful ways.

All of my ignorance and immaturity walked on by me when you, O Lord, were so merciful to me for me to see this day that I know You.

I am spiritually mature in doing Your will today, that You, O Lord, will not walk by me like you didn't do so real in all of my past years. You, O Lord, protected me from destroying myself unto death.

You, O Lord, didn't walk by me from sun up to sun down day after day — even though I was a wanderer who wandered through the pages of the book of my life.

You kept me on your bookshelf of love.

You, my Lord and Savior Jesus Christ, have never walked by me and left me in my broken life. Even though I broke it to pieces and didn't search to find You with all of my heart.

I had walked by You many times, O Lord. You called out to me but I ignored your call to chase behind a world of sin that would have killed me if you, my Lord, weren't a dear friend to me.

You, O Lord, didn't walk by me when disappointments and heartaches walked by me to leave me in my sorrows.

You, O Lord, took my hand and pulled me along life's rocky trails. It was in Your plan to save my soul.

Live For

Criminals live to hurt people.

True Christians live for treating people right.

Criminals live for killing people.

True Christians live for saving people's souls.

Criminals live for robbing people.

True Christians live for giving to people.

Criminals live for disrespecting people.

True Christians respect all people.

Criminals live for lying to people.

True Christians live for telling the truth to all people.

Criminals live for causing people to suffer.

True Christians live to bear people's burdens.

Criminals live for hating people.

True Christians live for loving people.

A true Christian is loving and obeying Jesus Christ.

Can't Compare Jesus

We can't compare Jesus with Adam.

We can't compare Jesus with Enoch.

We can't compare Jesus with Noah.

We can't compare Jesus with Abraham.

We can't compare Jesus with Isaac.

We can't compare Jesus with Jacob.

We can't compare Jesus with Joseph.

We can't compare Jesus with Moses.

We can't compare Jesus with Joshua.

We can't compare Jesus with Elijah.

We can't compare Jesus with King David.

We can't compare Jesus with Job.

We can't compare Jesus with Isaiah.

We can't compare Jesus with Jeremiah.

We can't compare Jesus with Ezekiel.

We can't compare Jesus with Daniel.

We can't compare Jesus with Amos.

We can't compare Jesus with Haggai.

We can't compare Jesus with any of the prophets and kinds. They were all born in sin except for Jesus, who was born without sin.

Jesus created them all and was before them all to have no end.

We Can't Judge the Truth

We can't speak the truth to some people who will say we are judging them.

We can't judge the truth on any day. The truth is what it is, what has happened and what is going on.

We can't form our opinions about the truth that is real to set us free from lies.

If we see people doing wrong and speaking about it, some will say we are judging them.

We can't judge the truth.

Many people won't like to hear the truth any time, but their opinions can't change the truth. This is just done by people who love to tell lies. They will hold a grudge against anyone who tells the truth.

The Pharisees tried to judge Jesus Christ, who is the truth, the way and the life.

The truth will judge anyone who breaks God's commandments that wicked people hate to keep.

The truth will never make a mistake when judging our sins, but we can make mistakes in judging even our blood kin.

Our Hereditary Tendencies

Our hereditary tendencies can be sinful. We can inherit some sins from our parents, who had sinful hereditary tendencies from their parents.

We have some good and bad hereditary tendencies in our flesh, no matter how good we are.

Hereditary tendencies can be like an unsolved mystery that is far from being solved, especially for those who are born without both of their parents in their lives.

They won't know without a doubt about what their absent parent is really like, but will inherit some of their good ways and bad ways so real.

We all have some hereditary tendencies of good and bad habits that may stand out upon the land.

Jesus had nothing but good hereditary tendencies from his virgin mother.

Jesus was born without sin under the sun.

Jesus didn't inherit his mother's bad hereditary tendencies. His heavenly Father wouldn't allow His son to have anything bad.

He allowed his son to be our Lord and savior at a great risk that he took on for you and me to be saved.

For as Long as You Live

For as long as you live it's not too late to treat people right in the winter's chill and in the summer's heat.

For as long as you live it's not too late to change for the better, even if your life looks disarranged.

For as long as you live it's not too late to help someone to be saved.

For as long as you live it's not too late to give someone a helping hand or buy them a meal.

For as long as you live it's not too late to do some good things, even if you are locked up in prison and many people believe your life is through.

For as long as you live it's not too late to confess and repent of your sins unto Jesus Christ who will give you and me the best that's yet to come when he comes back again.

For as long as you live it's not too late to choose to live for Jesus before the end.

Getting More and More

Many people are getting more and more material things, so as it seems.

Many people are getting more and more foolish to do anything that they put their minds on.

Many people are getting more and more dreams that they want to come true.

Many people are getting more and more smarter by going to college and getting high GPA scores.

Many people are getting more and more wicked. We can see it on the news when they're talking about crime being a lot more than a little bit out of control.

Many people are getting more and more sick. The hospitals are so filled up with sick people who we just don't know.

Many people are getting more and more greedy for money. They are over-working themselves and not spending any time with their honey. They're making big profits throughout the land.

Many people are getting more and more rich and have so much money in the bank that it makes it easier to make more and more friends.

Many people are getting poorer and poorer. They have nothing at all. Many people are born poor and will stay poor no matter whether they're short or tall, big or small.

Only a few people will get more and more close to Jesus Christ and know that everything in life is so vain if Jesus didn't pay our price.

God's Love

The sunlight will ray God's love all day long.

The full white moon will glow God's love all night long.

The stars will sparkle God's love across the universe.

We can't say enough of God's love that will always treat us right and not wrong.

We can sing God's love all through the church where God's love will fulfill our ministry work.

We breathe God's love that gives us life to live to be all about doing God's holy will.

We smile God's love on our faces to cheer up a sad face to not fear sorrow that is not dear to anyone.

The sky opens wide to God's love to hover over all the living that will never have enough of needing God's love.

All around the world the great and small survive due to God's love in the summer, winter, spring and fall.

All things that exist are from God's love through his son, Jesus Christ who loves all creatures living off of God's love.

Just By

You can be a blessing to others just by being present in their eyesight.

You may not know why they are so glad to see you.

It's not always what you say to be a blessing to others who may not always see their way out of a bad situation.

It's not always what you do to be a blessing to others who might just be glad to see you again.

Just by the way you carry yourself you can surely be a blessing to someone else who will see Jesus living in you every time he or she sees you.

You can be a blessing to others just by the way you dress yourself before them. They will see you want to be all about doing God's will even in the way that you dress to give God your best.

Just by listening to others and giving them a smile you can be a blessing to others to go the extra mile when they feel like giving up.

You can be a blessing to others just by saying nothing at the right time.

Jesus said nothing before some of his accusers who just wanted to catch Him in a lie.

Just by looking at people some may feel your hatred or your love.

There is No Jealousy in Love

A man has to let his wife talk to other men.

He will do that if he respects her and trusts her for no jealousy can come into his heart.

A woman has to let her husband talk to other women without getting jealous.

If a husband and wife put their trust in the Lord, they will trust one another when they see each other talking to the opposite sex.

There is no jealousy in love. The more you love your spouse for who he or she is, the more you will know that love is freedom and not being kept in bondage.

Jesus will let us talk to who we want to talk to, even though he may feel left out.

Jesus gave us a free will from his love for us.

A man cannot impose his will upon his wife. If he does, he doesn't trust her.

A woman cannot impose her will upon her husband who must love her to love himself.

There is no jealousy in love.

The free will is exercised in love that is God from heaven above.

A man can't make his wife love him and a woman can't make her husband love her.

Love is from free will each and every day.

There is no jealousy in love.

Jealousy is from selfishness that wants to control the husband and wife and make them not be who they are in the marriage wherever they go.

God's jealousy is not selfishness. Man's jealousy can be selfish.

No One but Jesus is Perfect

No one but Jesus is perfect. Jesus will never make a mistake in word and in deed for you and me to be saved.

I will not say all the right words and you will not say all the right words day after day.

I will not do all the right things and you will not do all the right things in the winter, spring, summer and fall.

No one but Jesus Christ is perfect. Our lord and savior gives us a ministry for us to labor in spreading his gospel.

You and I can always be ourselves with Jesus, who is perfect to always see us for who we are.

We can't always be ourselves with people who can misunderstand us and take us the wrong way, like a spouse can do.

No one but Jesus is perfect. We can always have a relationship with Him and never get let down at any time, or wonder about whether He will change for the worst on us.

No one but Jesus is perfect. We should always love Him first and above everyone we love on earth.

The Lord Has Given

The Lord has given you and me something to bless people's lives. It depends on whether we use it for good or evil.

We all have something good from the Lord, who is the best of the best above everyone else.

You and I should always use our good for the Lord, who gives us good gifts to glorify and magnify His holy name that will always lift us up to do good things.

The Lord gives everyone something good to bless someone else.

Everyone under the sun will not use the good to bless someone else's life.

So many people will use their good for the wrong reasons. That's something Jesus Christ our Lord hates to see.

We will reap what we sow. If we sow the good that the Lord gives us we will reap the good from our heads down to our toes.

The Lord has given you and me something good to not keep to ourselves. We will get blessed if we use the good to bless others who belong to the Lord just like you and me.

If You Don't Have Jesus

You could have a beautiful house and a beautiful car but what does it all mean if you don't have Jesus in your heart?

You could have a good job and plenty of money in the bank but what does it all mean if you don't have Jesus who will never leave your life blank?

You could have great success and accomplish your dreams but what does it all mean if you don't have Jesus to be redeeded?

You could be in great health and travel around the world but what does it all mean if you don't have Jesus who is beyond the gates of pearls?

You could have good friends and live in a good neighborhood but what does it all mean if you don't love Jesus like you should?

You could be a genius and be great in life but what does it all mean if you don't have Jesus Christ in your life?

You could be very talented and have a lot of things but what does it mean if you don't have Jesus who the holy angels sing songs about forever and ever?

You could be a good person and help people but if you don't have Jesus you will be in the depths of being lost in your sins.

If you and I don't have Jesus, that is a sin.

There are People

There are people who will say whatever comes to their minds without thinking that what they're saying may not be on time.

There are people who will do whatever they want to do without thinking about it all the way through.

There are people who don't care about what they say and believe it will have no bad effect on you and me.

There are people who don't care about what they do and don't want to stop doing what they want to do. They don't care that they have a bad effect on you and me.

Jesus would always say words of truth to set people free from lies.

Jesus always cared about what he did in the eyes of people. Jesus did nothing but good things even when He ordered the merchants to get out of His temple. What they were doing was bad to buy and sell animals in His house of prayer.

You Watched Over Me

O Lord, you watched over me when I was a little child.

O Lord, you protected me from the worst kinds of things that were so vile.

You, O Lord, smiled down on me, even though I had experienced some bad things in my life.

You, O Lord, still watched over me who has never seen you. You never let the devil into my life so he could make it a failure and be over.

O Lord, you watched over me when I was drunk and sober.

You, my Lord Jesus Christ, watched over me today so that I can say thank you, my Lord, for protecting me in so many ways that I never see.

No one can ever be a better watchman than You, O Lord, who truly sees my past, present and future life.

You watch over me as if I was the only one who needs to be saved in You.

Jesus Will Always See

We don't always see what is good for us.

Jesus will always see, and that we can trust.

We don't always see what needs to be done.

Jesus will always see with the victory that He won.

We don't' always see what is ahead of us.

Jesus will always see from dusk till dawn.

We don't always see what will happen next.

Jesus will always see and surely let us know.

We don't' always see who is our enemy.

Jesus will always see our enemy, who's not worth a penny.

We don't always see who is against us.

Jesus will always see to crush dislike and hatred.

We don't always see where we are going.

Jesus will always see where He will take you and me.

Love Is

Love is not about how you feel at the spur of the moment. That can go away so real.

Love is about getting to know that person for who they are.

Love is not about being caught up in the heat of the moment.

Love is about taking the time to be friends.

Love is not about meeting someone for the first time and believing that someone is right for you. The attraction can decline as soon as you meet someone else who looks so fine and is so kind.

Love is not about talking a good talk to someone day to day.

Love is not about winning someone's affection.

Love is about letting someone in your heart to know what direction you want to go with them.

Love is not about doing good things in the church.

Love is about loving Jesus Christ, who will never hurt your heart and will never change on you.

Love is not about holding church positions that you and I can do.

Love is about holding onto Jesus Christ even if the church pews are numbered down to a few.

Your Human Rights

If you want to know your human rights, read the bible that is full of human rights and is always reliable.

The Pharisees tried to take away Jesus' human rights to teach the truth to the people day after day.

Jesus used his human rights to heal the sick, cast out demons, feed the hungry and do many other miracles in people's eyesight.

Jesus taught about the rights of all people to believe in Him and be saved.

Many of the Jews tried to deceive the gentiles to make them believe that the Jews had more human rights to be saved in the Lord.

The Lord let the gentiles know that He came to this world to save them from their sins before it's too late.

God had used Moses to let King Pharaoh know that His people who were slaves had the same human rights to be free to live a prosperous life.

If you want to know your human rights, read the bible and see Jesus Christ giving human rights to all men to be saved through the price He paid.

I Didn't Grow Up Knowing a Lot of Truth

I didn't grow up knowing a lot of truth that I am so blessed to know today, especially about Jesus Christ, my Lord, who is my best friend.

I didn't grow up knowing a lot of truth about my life that wandered through the past years when I didn't know Jesus Christ.

It's a miracle to me to know a lot of truth, especially from the bible that I didn't read for my mind to be gone in the wind.

It's a miracle that the Lord has brought me this far to know a lot of truth that is so good for my heart.

I've never felt so free in all of my life because knowing a lot of truth has set me free from a lot of lies that knocked me down in so much sin.

I didn't know a lot of truth for a long time.

I am so glad that Jesus winked his eye at my ignorance that Jesus used to define me to be so helpless to lies that were told to me.

I am so happy to know a lot of truth today that I truly see the light of God's holy word shining through my soul.

I didn't grow up knowing a lot of truth that many people had closed the door of their hearts to.

They know a lot of truth and didn't live by it.

All the truth is doing God's holy will that is written in His word of truth through his holy spirit.

It is all truth about Jesus Christ, who is the living root of all existence all through eternity.

Jesus Wants Our Prayers from Our Hearts

We can't practice how to pray to Jesus, who wants our prayers from our hearts that you and I need to give to Him.

We can't dress up our prayers to Jesus Christ, who wants our prayers from our hears so He can bless our lives.

We can't pretend when we pray to Jesus, who wants our prayers to be from our hearts and true to Him every second, minute and hour of the day.

We can't be doubtful when we pray to Jesus, who wants our prayers from our hearts so the Holy Spirit can take our prayers up through the ozone layers.

We can't be living in sin and believe that Jesus will hear our prayers from an evil heart. We must have a repentant heart so very near to Jesus, who wants our prayers from our hearts of love and obedience every day.

We can't deceive Jesus when we pray to Him. He knows our motives in every way.

Jesus wants our prayers from a pure heart. We can't pray to Jesus with a selfish heart. Jesus wants our prayers from a selfless heart; those he will answer.

We can't pray to Jesus with an untrustworthy heart from the start of the day to the end of the day. Jesus wants a trustworthy heart.

We must pray to Jesus with a bold heart and not a fearful heart. Jesus will guard a bold heart that a little child can have to amaze Jesus Christ, the Son of God.

If Life was Always Easy to Live

If life was always easy to live, we wouldn't need Jesus, who always did his heavenly Father's will when Jesus lived on earth without sin.

Every day will not be an easy day for you and me, who will especially live our lives unto Jesus who we don't always fully trust.

If life was always easy to live, we would have no disappointments and sorrows to encourage us to hold onto Him today when tomorrow is not promised to you and me.

If life was always easy to live we would be happy all the time and would have no problems for us to be filled with perfection in our lives.

Jesus Christ, our lord and savior, was the only perfect human being. Jesus had all of God's favor, even though his life wasn't always easy to live among sinners who He died for and rose from the grave to save from sin.

If life was always easy to live, no one would ever feel down and out of hope. Jesus didn't leave anyone out of His saving grace and salvation. Jesus is our only hope in this life that's not always easy to live day after day.

Many church folds don't always trust the Lord, who will not let us sink like a boat if we live our lives unto Him.

Not Wise

Many people are smart and bright, but are not wise and make bad choices.

Many people have a very high IQ but are not wise and do foolish things.

Whoever doesn't believe in Jesus Christ the king of kings is not wise.

Many people have a lot of head knowledge but are not wise because they don't use their knowledge for something good around the clock.

Many people are very talented but are not wise because they don't use their talents for the Lord.

Many people are skillful in doing things but are not wise in doing the right things unto the Lord, who has no end for doing right things.

Many people are creative with ideas and inventions but are not wise because they don't keep God's commandments, even if their intentions are good.

It's not wise for anyone to not love God the Father, the Son and the Holy Ghost, who is wise beyond our hearts, minds, and souls.

We all need wisdom from the Lord to make wise choices.

God Doesn't Control Anyone

A lot of people in this world love to control other people and make them do what they want. God doesn't control anyone, no matter what anyone says.

A lot of people in this world love to control whoever they can and be their master. God doesn't control anyone's mind and leaves us free to think every day.

A lot of people love to control other people and make them bow down to them. God doesn't control anyone's life or make them worship Him on holy ground.

A lot of people love to control other people and make them do everything they say. God doesn't control anyone or make them do his will that is holy day after day.

A lot of people love to control other people and make them believe what they believe. God doesn't control anyone or make them believe in His son, who loves to relieve you and me of the slavery of sin.

A lot of people love to control other people and make them say what they want them to say. God doesn't control anyone or make them say what He wants them to say all through the day and night.

A lot of people love to be in control all through their lives. God doesn't control anyone or make them give Him the glory and praise that the holy angels will always do.

God doesn't control any of his holy angels in heaven above.

God is love and love is God, who will never control anyone or force them to love Him. There is no control in love.

On Mere Human Intelligence

On mere human intelligence people can only create things that will sooner or later wear out and break down.

On mere human intelligence people will believe in what they see, but that is temporary.

On mere human intelligence you an I will not know about spiritual things to be eternal beyond physical things.

On mere human intelligence physical science is of the naked eyesight.

Our free will choice is of God, who made an alliance with man through his son, Jesus Christ, who created all things beyond physical science, which is from the ideas of men.

From sun up to sun down On mere human intelligence people will fail to be amazed by the wisdom of God, who is the ancient of days beyond the atheists' false ideas of believing that life on earth has been here for millions of years.

God is the first one to exist and will not allow sin to exist for millions of years.

On mere human intelligence people's senses will have no clear focus on God's wisdom being forever above the intelligence of mankind and womankind, which is still existing through God's love from his Son, whose intelligence is perfect beyond time.

The truth of God's holy word is above human intelligence because we are not all-knowing like God, whose Holy Spirit is beyond mere human intelligence.

Our Faith in Jesus Christ

Our faith in Jesus Christ will not convince everybody to believe in Jesus. It will always make good sense to have faith in Jesus, who only a fool wouldn't believe in.

Our faith in Jesus Christ won't make us be without sin. We were born in sin and must confess and repent.

Our faith in Jesus Christ will not encourage all men, women, boys and girls to deny self and follow Jesus Christ.

Our faith in Jesus Christ will cause us to have many enemies in our lives. Many people don't care to hear anything about our faith in Jesus, until they are on their deathbeds and want the power of Jesus to revive and heal their dying bodies.

Our faith in Jesus Christ will show and tell in our lives for the people of the world to see that we are different from them. They will see that we love to talk about Jesus, who we don't see and who they don't see. The people of the world will always talk about who they see and what they see.

Our faith in Jesus Christ is something that we will never regret, no matter what anyone says.

Beyond All

Beyond all of our best dreams there is a heaven that Jesus will take us to.

Beyond all of our questions there is a heaven that Jesus Christ will take us to one day if we are saved in Him in this life.

Beyond all the good deeds we do there is a heaven that Jesus will take us to.

Beyond all who we see and what we see there is a heaven that Jesus will take us to if you and I love Him and obey His ten golden rules.

Beyond all of the good words we say there is a heaven that Jesus will take us to one day when he comes back again, just like the bible says.

Beyond all that is in this world there is a heaven that Jesus will take us to and that perfect place is very real.

Beyond all of our accomplishments and failures there is a heaven for us.

Beyond all of our suffering and pain there is a heaven beyond the graveyard dust.

Being Wise

Being wise can save us from injury and pain, and being wise is believing in Jesus' name.

Being wise can save us from a heartache and being wise can make us spiritually mature in Jesus Christ.

Being wise can save our lives and being wise can keep us from strife.

Being wise can make us think twice to keep us from doing something wrong.

Being wise can cause us to live a long life.

The beginning of being wise is to love Jesus, who cannot lie to us about His commandments being good, holy, perfect and righteous for all to keep in every neighborhood.

Memories

Memories have a place of their own to go to. They're what is seen all through the years of you and me living right or wrong.

Some memories are not good to watch in our minds, that long for good memories to hold onto.

Memories are like the stars in the night, they can sparkle so bright.

Memories can be like a good or bad movie we watch in our minds.

Memories are a shadow of what was real in our lives.

Memories can go here and there in our minds.

When some people get old, they will not remember the loved ones who were in their lives.

Memories are not always kind to everyone.

Memories can vanish, especially from senior citizen's minds when they have memory loss day after day.

The best way to sharpen our memories is to study God's holy word that the Holy Spirit can always bring to our minds.

We won't have to sweat to memorize these words and believe in Jesus Christ, who the bible reveals to us.

Memories will put our trust in Jesus and help our minds to get filled with His holy light.

If We

If we don't love Jesus, we will do just about anything that's not right to do without a doubt.

If we don't love Jesus, we will believe just about anything that is not true and get deceived.

If we don't love Jesus, we will say just about anything that is not good day after day.

If we love Jesus, we will deny ourselves and pick up our cross and follow Him who paid our cost.

If we love Jesus, we will get rid of our pride and let Jesus be our guide.

If we love Jesus, we will love our neighbors and do them no harm or put them in danger throughout their lives.

If we love Jesus, we will keep His ten commandments day after day under the sun, stars and moon lit rays.

God's Ways

God's ways are miraculous each and ever day.

God's ways give us life to live under the sunlight rays.

Our ways can be selfish and we can do one another wrong in some kind of way. That makes us weak and not strong in the Lord, Jesus Christ.

God's ways are always right and about doing things that Jesus did when He lived on earth and brought the word of God and God's ways of doing things to the world.

Our ways can change and we may not even see it until someone tells us.

God's ways will not sit back and let the devil have his way with us.

The bible says God will not put on us more than we can bear.

God's ways are always holy, good and perfect here and there and everywhere.

Our ways are not always good and God knows that — it's not rare.

The Lord is Always on Time

The Lord is always on time to show us what we need to see.

The Lord is always on time to protect you and me from harm and danger.

The Lord is always on time to help you and me take the first step.

The Lord is always on time to be there for us.

No one else is always on time; that we can trust.

The Lord is always on time to get our minds on Him who is always so divine.

The Lord is always on time to pick us up when we fall down into sin that would want us all to be too late to be saved in Jesus Christ, our Lord.

The Lord is always on time to renew our lives to live doing His holy will.

The Lord is always on time to shine His holy light in our hearts day after day.

It's Never Good

It's never good to pick on people. No one is better than anyone else upon the land.

It's never good for a man to show off his authority over people as if he is better than those who are under him. The Lord sees every motive and Jesus can show someone's bad motives to you and me.

It's never good to make fun of people who belong to the Lord.

It's never good to let your feelings run wild on people. We need to be careful about what we say, especially to someone who sees no need to listen. Jesus is always there to listen to what we have to say. He can always bear to take it in.

It's never good to cause someone to stumble or fall away from the Lord. Jesus Christ, our Lord, is all about building us up in His church that He is the head of.

It's never good to get offended by the truth that's spoken in love to help us learn from our mistakes.

It's never good to get revenge and it's never good to be envious of someone who the Lord may have his hands upon. He blesses you and me.

So Smart

Many people are so smart and can talk with plenty of good sense, but they will believe what is not true with good intent.

The devil has made many people believe that a lie is true.

Many people are so smart and will let something that doesn't make any good sense get by them because they believe what is not real is real.

The devil is so much smarter than you and me, no matter how smart we are. The devil can deceive us if we don't know God's holy word and don't believe in Jesus Christ, who is forevermore smarter than the devil.

So many people are on a very high educational level and will believe that the bible is not true.

Many people in the bible were so smart but were living in their sins.

Many people are so smart with a lot of head knowledge and will believe that the truth is a lie and that a lie is the truth.

By the Choices You Make

You can know who you are by the choices you make.

Make Jesus your choice this very day.

You can know how smart you are by the choices you make.

Make Jesus your choice and be saved.

You can know how good you are by the choices you make.

Make Jesus your choice in God's amazing grace.

You can know how bad you are by the choices you make.

Make Jesus your choice before it's too late.

You can know your destiny by the choices you make.

Make Jesus your choice to be destined to heaven and not hell.

The choices you make can show and tell on you so very well.

Make Jesus Christ your choice because He will never fail you.

You can know how foolish you are by the choices you make.

Make Jesus your choice to be wise all through your life.

So Poor When It Comes to Spiritual Things

Many people are rich with material things but are so poor when it comes to spiritual things that they don't have behind their doors.

Many people are well off with material things but are so poor when it comes to spiritual things that will bring us spiritual riches.

Many people are working so much to get a lot of material things but are so poor when it comes to spiritual things from the Lord

Many people are getting more and more spiritually poor and getting more and more material things that are so temporary.

Spiritual things are eternal in the Lord who always knows that eternal riches will never rust or erode and will never pass away.

We can take eternal riches with us to the grave if we are saved in Jesus Christ.

We can't take material things with us to the grave, where material things won't do us any good. The dead don't know to care about having material things.

Jesus can bless us with spiritual things and material things that belong to Him who can take both away if we are doing Him so wrong each and every day.

Means Something

A blank sheet of paper means something for it means that you can write on it so as it seems.

A picture in a frame means something for it means that you can look at it for a long time, no matter where you live.

A candlestick means something for it means that you can light it to see in a dark room.

What we plan means something for it means that you want to do something and follow through with it.

A stairway means something for it means that you can walk up and down on it day after day.

A man means something for he means to live above the ground and love and obey Jesus Christ.

A woman means something for she means to live her life to love and obey Jesus Christ.

A boy and a girl mean something for they mean to love and obey Jesus Christ, the lord of lords.

Jesus means every good thing for all men, women, boys and girls.

We mean something to Jesus.

To believe in Him is to be saved from a sinful world.

I Would be a Fool to Keep My Eyes on People

I would be a fool to keep my eyes on people who have a sinful nature and let me down.

I would be a fool to keep my eyes on people who have a sinful nature and lie to me and believe they are better than me.

I would be a fool to keep my eyes on people who have a sinful nature and are jealous of me.

I would be a fool to keep my eyes on people who have a sinful nature and do me wrong.

I would be a fool to keep my eyes on people who have a sinful nature and turn against me.

I would be a fool to keep my eyes on people who have a sinful nature and talk about about me.

I would be a fool to keep my eyes on people who have a sinful nature and judge me.

I would be a fool to not keep my eyes on my Lord and savior, Jesus Christ, who is perfect without sin and will always bless my life.

It's Nothing New Today

Many people have turned their backs on the Lord after He brought them out of a bad situation. It's nothing new today without a doubt.

Many people back in the bible days turned their backs on the Lord after He brought them out of a bad situation. They didn't see their way out.

It's nothing new today that many people will act like they don't remember where they come from and turn their backs on the Lord.

Many people back in the bible days acted like they didn't remember where they came from, surely being some hard days that the Lord brought them out of.

Today, many people have turned their backs on the Lord like Peter did back in the bible days. Peter acted like he never knew Jesus was treated badly by his enemies that crucified Him.

What happened back in the bible days is nothing new today in our eyes. We are only repeating, in many ways, what happened back then.

It's nothing new today. Just like back in the bible days we have problems whether we are great or small.

It's nothing new today that people have real problems upon the land.

We all need the Lord today like the people needed the Lord back in the bible days.

O Lord, You Always Know

O Lord, You always know what is best for me. I don't always know what is best for me to be relieved from stress.

O Lord, You always know what I can bear. I don't always know what I can bear here and there.

O Lord, You always know me better than I know myself.

I don't always know myself or anyone else.

O Lord, You always know what I will say.

I don't always know what I will say, even to this day.

O Lord, You always know what I will do.

I don't always know what I will do and can break Your golden rules.

O Lord, You always know what I will think.

I don't always know what I will think and that may cause my mind to sink down in sin.

O Lord, You always know my heart.

I don't always know my heart that can fall apart in heartache and grief if I don't surrender it to You.

Changeable Ways

You can't trust people who have changeable ways. They will say one thing and then they'll change what they say.

You can't trust people who have changeable ways. They will say one thing and will not do what they say.

You can't trust people who have changeable ways. They can make you believe that they love you today, tomorrow and forever … until you need their help.

You can't trust people who have changeable ways. They can melt your heart with their kind words and make you believe they accept you for who you are, then they will change on you and act like you don't exit.

We can be thankful that Jesus is not changeable. He doesn't say one thing and then change it. We can be so thankful that Jesus is not changeable with His ways that are surely His will for us to do every day.

Jesus will always love us. He will never change on you or me or cause us to not trust Him.

The ways of Jesus are the same forever and evermore.

Changeable people will turn against you in some kind of way and ignore you and keep their distance if they believe they can't trust you and me.

Jesus is the way of truth and will never change his love — it will always be the same.

We all have some changeable ways because we were born with a sinful nature upon our names.

We Must Look at Jesus

We must look at Jesus and not at the mountain of the bad things we are up against that can seem so non-stop.

We must look at Jesus and not look at the valley of obstacles that Jesus can make to flow down his brook and disappear.

We must look at Jesus and not look at the storm of stress that Jesus can calm down around the clock.

We must look at Jesus and not look at the flood of worry that can make our blood pressure rise in a hurry. Jesus can dry up the flood and make the ground of your life hard again so you can reach a higher level.

We must look at Jesus Christ our Lord and savior and not look at anyone who shows favor to material things over Jesus who is eternal.

We should always look at His holy word, it is the truth to set us free no matter where we live.

Proud People

Proud people love to say I am this and I am that, no matter where they live at.

Proud people love to show off what they have and love to show off what they can do with their hands

Proud people love to say I am doing this and I have done that a long time ago before you were born from your mother's womb.

Proud people love to speak very highly about themselves and make themselves look important wherever they go.

Proud people love to talk about the things of the world and not about who created this world.

Proud people like to doubt the Lord Jesus Christ and fail to realize that day after day, God's grace is running out.

The Best Kind of People

The best kind of people in this world are Christians, but everyone who goes to church doesn't obey the holy law of God.

Every true Christian knows that believing in Jesus Christ is truly loving him and our neighbors.

Every true Christian will always do the labor work of love. The worst kind of people in the world are murderers who love to kill men, women, boys and girls.

Jesus gave up his life on the cross for murderers to turn away from their sins and believe in Him even though they still have to pay for their terrible crimes.

No one has any right to kill anyone at any time of the day and night.

There are only two kinds of people in this world: the righteous and the wicked.

The righteous are the best kind of people to have around day after day.

No one is worse than a cold-blooded killer who loves to take people down to the grave and believe it's the right thing to do.

The best kind of people in this world are Christians who won't kill anyone except in self-defense, which the Lord won't hold them accountable for.

The Slavery that Gives Us Freedom

We can be a slave to living a righteous life. That will give us freedom in our Lord and savior Jesus Christ.

When Jesus was resurrected from the grave, he gave the whole world the freedom to be saved in Him.

We can choose to not be a slave to sin. It has no power over us because we can be a new creature in Jesus right at this very hour.

Jesus gives us the power to live a righteous life.

The slavery that gives us freedom is to obey God's holy law through the price that Jesus paid on the cross for our sins.

There is only one kind of slavery that gives us the freedom over living in sin because of the love of God, who gave us his only begotten son.

The old creature that we were was a slave unto sin. The new creature that you and I become is a slave in living right by God who gives us freedom from living in sin.

The slavery that gives us freedom is righteous living under the sun.

The Answer

Only the Lord has the answer to all of our problems. He can solve them for us to truly see.

Only the Lord has the answer to everything that is going on in this world that no president, king or religious leader can make perfect to have no sins.

Only the Lord has the answer to whatever goes on in our lives from day to day.

The Lord's answer is in His holy word that Jesus says: If you love Me, you will keep My commandments.

Keeping God's commandments is the answer to every nation's problems. People in every nation should do God's holy will every day. That way, the devil can't force anyone to sin against God.

Only the Lord Jesus Christ has the answer to the way we should live. Surely, keeping His commandments is the answer so real.

There is no other answer to this world's problems, no matter how we feel.

We Can't Leave Jesus Out of Life

We can't leave Jesus out of life, for Jesus is the life to live day after day, and that life is real.

Jesus lived a sinless life here on earth to show us the right way to live our lives so we can't leave Him out of our lives.

Many people will come up with many ways to live their lives not like the bible says to live.

Everybody's heart is not with the Lord Jesus Christ, who created life and gave up His life to pay our price.

We can't leave Jesus out of life, because only a fool would do that. But, when he or she is dying, they may very well realize life in its fullest by calling on the name of Jesus in their last breath.

Jesus rose from the grave where death couldn't keep him in the grave or the tomb.

Life comes from Jesus who engineered life in the womb of a mother who will birth a baby with life.

Death can't get rid of life that will be here when Jesus comes back again with life eternal through God's love.

So Unexpected

A loved one can die so unexpected that we don't see it coming our way.

The pain we feel can be like a shockwave hitting us so unexpected.

Jesus always sees for us to trust Him to get us through the unexpected.

If our loved ones get sick, we will usually see if they will die or not die from the sickness.

If someone gets killed or commits suicide, it can be so unexpected that just cannot hide from you and me.

Only the Lord can always get us through the unexpected that can surely catch us off guard and cause us to be so lost in the woods.

Things can happen so unexpected upon this sinful land.

Jesus Christ didn't come to this world unexpected to save us from our sins. His mercy and grace was never unexpected for the world to embrace.

Can Use You

Someone may try to use you for financial support and will want you to be a good sport about being used.

Someone may try to use you for emotional support and will want a big hug or a handshake, while knowing they won't change for the better.

Someone may try to use you to say good words about them, even though they know what they're asking you to say isn't true.

Someone may try to use you to do something bad for him or her, and will feel good about using you.

Do you and I ever try to use the Lord by praying and asking Him for something and telling Him we will change if He answers our prayers?

The Lord can answer our prayers and we may not keep our word to Him, but He understands us better than we will ever understand ourselves. We won't always see that we are trying to use the Lord.

We can never plot to try to use the Lord. He will never let anyone use Him. He can always stop you and me in our tracks by not answering our prayers if our reasons are wrong.

Under the Sun, Moon and Stars

Under the sun, moon and stars, aging is a common thing. We will all cross over that bridge.

Birds love to sing when life will not always sing us a happy song under the sun, moon and stars.

Time can treat us so wrong and can fail us, letting us die before our time under the sun, moon and stars.

We can't always define the meaning of why God allows some good young people to die before their time under the sun, moon and stars.

Someone can walk or drive by your house today, and the next day they may be far gone into the black hole of death under the sun, moon and stars.

Under the sun, moon and stars no one can fully know the whole heart that can cause heartaches, jealousy, pride, greed, wars and death.

God's only begotten son came down from heaven where Jesus left all of his eternal riches to be born in the flesh without sin.

Under the sun, moon and stars life is like a shadow that passes away in the morning light.

God created us all and we can't say that something else created us under the sun, moon and stars.

The sun, moon and stars won't deny that when a fool can believe that there is no God to trust.

If Jesus is Not in It

That old wolf, the devil, will surely blow your house down if Jesus is not in it to show and tell on your children misbehaving so badly.

If you try to build your house on your own, that old wolf, the devil, will blow it down to be shown in the eyesight of others.

If Jesus is in your house, it doesn't mean that you will never have any problems with your spouse and your children.

If Jesus is in your house, things will get better and not worse so it seems to anyone who lets Jesus build their house every day.

That old wolf, the devil, will surely blow your house down in ways you don't see coming because the devil is all about destroying your house no matter what educational level you are at.

If Jesus Christ is not in it, your house will stress you out and leave your life so empty and without peace.

Let Jesus build your house and you will never regret it. You'll have many more peaceful days ahead of you.

Why Should You Worship?

Why should you worship a human being who has sins and will one day die and be out of your life? Is it to make the devil grin?

Why should you worship nature when you can't pray to nature and get your prayers answered on any day?

Why should you worship material things that can wear out and breakdown in your hands?

Why should you worship temporary things that will one day pass away under the heavens that are forever real?

Why should you worship yourself when you can make a mistake and never hide it from Jesus, who is never too late to save you if you repent of your sins and believe in Him?

Why should you worship this world that is no friend to you from the day you were born until the day you die under the sun?

Why should you worship any kind of creature that can't give you life after death like Jesus will do when he comes back again to take you to heaven if you worship Him who can save you from your sins?

It's Hard

It's hard to be happy for someone else if you are not happy within yourself.

It's hard to encourage someone else if you are not encouraged within yourself.

It's hard to love someone else if you don't love yourself.

It's hard to pick someone else up if you are falling down.

It's hard to believe someone else's dream if you don't have a dream.

It's hard to give someone else something good if you don't enjoy the good things you have.

It's hard to be lost in your sins if you repent and believe in Jesus Christ to be saved before your life ends.

Our Faith in the Lord is Being Tested

Our faith in the Lord is being tested in some kind of way each and every day.

Our faith in the Lord is being tested by what we say.

Our faith in the Lord is being tested by the clothes that we wear as we go here and as we go there.

Our faith in the Lord is being tested by what we eat and by what we drink day after day and week after week.

Our faith in the Lord is being tested by the friends that we have day after day in this world.

Our faith in the Lord is being tested by the choices we make to show and tell on you and me.

Our faith in the Lord is being tested by the truth that we know, to do or not do wherever we go.

Our faith in the Lord is being tested in some kind of way, whether we know it or not in our moment in time.

Our faith in the Lord is being tested through the thick and thin of our lives until our lives come to an end.

Hopefully we will be saved in Jesus Christ, who can save us from our sins.

It's Not the Quantity, It's the Quality

It's not the quantity that can add up to nothing good. It's the quality that can surely be good like putting some good wood on a campfire.

There is a quantity of sinners when one saved sinner is the quality of God's amazing grace.

Many businesses are so concerned about the quantity of the products to be sold, but the many people who buy the products are concerned about the quality and whether it will last as it gets old.

Jesus doesn't care about the quantity of sins we have committed against Him. He truly cares about the quality of our repentance of sins and for us to be baptized and obey His golden rules.

It's not about the quantity that can be a lot of people going to church. It's the quality of whoever believes in Jesus Christ whose ministry work saves lost souls.

The quantity can add up to a lot of numbers to count in the church of God.

When the quality is our faith being as big as a mustard seed to the Lord, who is so deeply touched by our quality of love for Him and not by our quantity of good works that can't save us.

You Can't Please Everybody

You can't please everybody, even in the church where everybody may not be blessed by your ministry work.

Some people may say that your sermon was boring for them and they fell asleep as you tried to talk to them about the Lord.

Some people may say that your songs are all right but they aren't pleased to listen to them because it doesn't suit them with their walk with Jesus.

Some people may say they haven't read your published books and have no interest in what's inside them.

You can't please everybody or force them to say good things about you, no matter what good you do every day.

You can't please everybody, but pleasing the Lord is above whoever you can't please. No one can shut the door that God has opened for you to bless people's lives to be pleased by the good things you do in their eyes.

I Don't Want to Believe

I don't want to believe that I am better than someone else.

The Lord can bless my hands to get some success and the Lord can bring me down to ruin.

I don't want to be saying bad words to people and I don't want to be doing bad things to people.

The Lord can shut my mouth and can paralyze my body for me to surely know why.

I don't want to believe that I am all of this and all of that. The Lord can humble me no matter where I live.

I don't want to believe that I am always right about what I say and do.

The Lord can show me that my righteousness is like filthy rags day after day.

I don't want to believe that I have no sins.

The Lord can show me that I will break His laws until my life comes to an end.

I don't want to believe that my ministry work is more inspiring than someone else's ministry work in the church.

The Lord can take it away from me like I never had it before He gave it to me.

I don't want to believe that I can make excuses to the Lord.

The Lord won't fall for that on any day. He knows my heart in every way.

Love is Freedom

Love is freedom, love doesn't control anyone or make them love.

God is love from heaven above.

Love is freedom, love doesn't make anyone a slave.

It's His love that saves.

Love is freedom, love doesn't force anyone to love.

God gave us His only begotten son because of his love for us.

Love is freedom, love doesn't disobey law and order.

God is love across every border.

Love is freedom, love doesn't let us down.

God is love all around the world.

Love is freedom, love doesn't frown on sinners.

God is love to show no respect of persons on His holy ground.

Love is freedom, love is not unnatural and love won't ill or kill anyone.

God is love because God is freedom that He gives to us in His son, Jesus Christ, who sets us free for doing God's will that is also Jesus' will.

Go Back in the Past

Go back in the past to know that the Lord didn't let us die in our sins.

The Lord won't let anyone die in their sins before He opens their eyes to see and know the truth of His holy law.

Go back in the past to know that the Lord brought us all this far over our dreams and uncertain ways that were so flawed.

Go back in the past to give Jesus Christ the credit for sparing our lives through all of the strife and jealousy.

Go back in the past to know that Jesus supplied all of our needs when we were weak in our faith and prone to doing bad deeds.

Go back in the past and see Jesus' mercy and grace upon you and me as He brings us this far to be saved.

Go back in the past to know that Jesus didn't change His holy word that is also for our present and future and for us to believe in His holy name.

Go back in the past to know that Jesus carried us through the past years.

A fool loves to live in the past with no glory and praise unto Jesus who is always clear about saving our souls.

Jesus' Holy Name

Jesus' holy name can move the highest mountains and Jesus' holy name can purify the deepest ocean fountain.

Jesus' holy name is higher than the sun, moon and stars, and Jesus' holy name can heal all of our painful scars.

Jesus' holy name is deeper than the deep outer space, and Jesus' holy name will reach out to every place on earth.

Jesus' holy name will cause the angels to sing, and Jesus' holy name is greater than any president or king.

Jesus' holy name will cause the demons to tremble, and Jesus' holy name will cause us saint to assemble ourselves together in the church.

Jesus' holy name is the power of our ministry work, and Jesus' holy name is the answer to our soul search.

Only for a Short Time

We are here in the land of the living only for a short time.

The days, weeks, months, and years can seem to be a long time under the sun that shines down on our lives.

Our lifespan is short and many have their lives cut shorter, unable to survive an early grave.

Only for a short time are the years that we live that won't force us to do anything against our free will.

Jesus Christ, our Lord, lived a short life here on earth before he died on the cross and rose again to be our first choice over everyone else and over everything else in this world.

Many people live to get old, and remember their childhoods when they were little boys or little girls and didn't know that life can be short.

Only under the great blue sky is where life is short for all flesh and blood creatures that are prone to dying one day.

Jesus Christ is coming for the righteous living to be alive and never die.

We are here only for a short time in the land of living where living for Jesus is the greatest life to live.

Jesus will always bless our short lives for doing His will.

Created in the Image of God

Everybody is smart in some kind of way, and created in the image of God who is the true living God.

Everybody is creative in some kind of way, and created in the image of God, who is forever more powerful than any nation.

Everybody is talented in some kind of way, and created by God who created all boys, girls, women and men in his own image.

Everybody will sense something in some kind of way, because they are created in the image of God who is before all existence.

Everybody has the law of God in their hearts in some kind of way, and they were created in the image of God who is love.

Everybody has a mind, and was created in the image of God.

Everybody has a heart, and was created in the image of God who is not hard to love.

Everybody can be saved from their sins because they were created in the image of God who is a friend to all.

Even children who are born with a defect are created in the image of God and are loved by Him.

Everybody has free will, and was created in the image of God who gave us his only begotten son to keep us from being lost in sin if we make Jesus Christ our choice.

When I was a Little Child

When I was a little child, I did a lot of foolish things that were surely no good and nothing to sing about.

When I was a little child, I didn't know a lot of right from wrong; it was foreign to me.

When I was a little child, I didn't know what sin was, even though I was born in it.

I didn't know the Lord and savior Jesus Christ when I was a little child; that came later when I was an adult.

It's a miracle to even be allowed to grow up from a little child when there are so many young children who die young.

Life is not promised to even a little child. Only the Lord's reason is always right to permit a little child to die young.

My Lord and savior Jesus Christ was a little child without sin in his life.

Only Jesus never did anything foolish or wrong when he was a little child. He was the Son of God who lived so free from sin.

When I was a little child, Jesus knew me so perfectly even though I didn't know Him.

He brought me this far from a little child to an adult to live my life doing His holy will apart from my will that was like a sinking ship when I was a little child.

It's Wrong to be Thinking About

It's wrong to be thinking about saying something wrong that is not about Jesus Christ, who we all belong to every day.

It's wrong to be thinking about things that will separate us from Jesus, who we can always trust to give us the right thoughts to think about Him every day.

It's wrong to be thinking about leaning to our own ways of doing things. Jesus' ways of doing things are always right, even when the sun goes down and we lose its light.

It's wrong to be thinking about foolish things and evil things that will open the gate to death and hell upon our souls.

We need to always think about Jesus Christ being the king of kings and lord of lords. He will destroy death and hell one day.

It's wrong to be thinking about not being like Jesus Christ, who we can think about around the clock and never feel down and out. We know He is always right about everything.

It's Sin that Comes Out of the Closet

It's sin that comes out of the closet with something that is not natural to the naked eye.

It's sin that comes out of the closet with something that is not good to the naked eye.

The Lord hates our sins but loves you and me when we confess and repent our sins unto Him.

It's sin that comes out of the closet with a bad surprise to the naked eye.

The Lord God is not on our sides if we fully sin against Him and make excuses about it.

It's sin that comes out of the closet more times than a little bit to the naked eye.

The Lord Jesus Christ died for our sins and rose from the grave to give us victory over our sins from our heads to our toes.

It's sin that comes out of the closet with something bold to the naked eye.

Jesus has surely told us in His daily word that the wages of sin are death.

Whether it will be a fast death or a slow death, it's for sure that sin will leave us with nothing good.

Being Talked About

Is our faith in Jesus Christ being talked about in our neighborhoods where we can cause people to doubt that we love Jesus if we are living in sin?

Is our faith in Jesus being talked about on the job where we can rob the employer of the work we are supposed to do?

Is our faith in Jesus being talked about in the church where everyone's faith is not so strong in Jesus who we can hurt by not bearing one another's burdens, especially those who are weak in faith?

Our faith in Jesus Christ is being talked about for us to not always know how some people are deeply touched and trust that our faith in Jesus is real to them.

Is our faith in Jesus being talked about in this dim and dark world of sin that can't put out our light shining in Jesus Christ so very bright?

Many People

Many people will give the glory and praise to luck, instead of giving the glory and praise to Jesus, who is alive and not dead.

Many lives in danger are spared because of God's mercy and grace, not because of luck. Luck is only a word and can't save people's lives.

Only the Lord can hold back the angel of death; not luck, even though many people believe luck has the power to save lives. Luck is only useful to those who don't give the glory and praise to Jesus Christ, our Lord and savior, who forever lives beyond our days on earth that are short lived.

Many people believe in luck, but luck can't cleanse anyone from living in sin. Only Jesus can do that for me and you. We are not wise if we put luck above the Lord.

When your eyes see something that looks impossible, don't look to luck to make it possible. You can study the bible and see that Jesus makes the impossible possible.

Many people will give luck the glory and praise, but luck is not real and no one should put their faith in luck.

In the Shed of Our Hearts

We can put a lot of things in the shed in our back yard. We can fill that shed up with junk and make it hard to clean out.

We can put almost anything in the shed in our back yard. We can even take down a bed that we don't need and put it in the shed.

A shed can be useful to you and me, but we shouldn't put anything into the shed of our hearts.

Our hearts shouldn't be filled up with anything but Jesus Christ.

Jesus loves to fill up or sheds with the fruit of His spirit. He is all about love and we should be all about Jesus.

The shed in our back yard can get old, and the paint can fade away.

Only Jesus can keep the shed of our hearts looking brand new, if we love and obey Him all through our lives.

Jesus loves to get the junk that is sin out of the sheds of our hearts. He will eliminate it and make it fall apart.

It's Not So Easy

It's not so easy to publish a good book, especially when you want all the words to be spelled correctly and all the punctuation to be correct.

It's not so easy to create good songs. You want the music and message to be good so it lasts for a long time in people's minds.

It's not so easy to find a cure to heal all those who are sick in their beds waiting to be filled with hope.

It's not so easy to accomplish good things in this sinful world that loves to bring on failures upon you and me.

It's not so easy to get a good night's sleep when some neighbors are noisy in the neighborhood. They can even be some kinfolk who don't seem to care about whether you are well or sick.

It's not so easy to kick the dust off your feet and go somewhere else when you must love people's souls to be saved in Jesus Christ, especially your loved ones.

If We Love

If we love Jesus Christ, we will not intentionally sin against Him who loves us with no end.

If we love one another, we will try not to cause one another to sin against Jesus, who puts no pause on His love for us — His love for us is non-stop.

If we love Jesus, we will do His holy will according to His Ten Commandments holy law that is very real to keep from day to day.

If we love everyone, we will not try to cause anyone to sin against Jesus, who leaves no one out of His salvation to be saved in Him who is the Son of God.

If we love Jesus so truly, we will love one another so truly because we can't love Jesus without loving each other. We will know that love is not love without loving Jesus, wherever we go.

Who Can Suffer More than God?

Someone said, "Who can suffer more than God, who feels everyone's heartache and grief from the start of the day to the end of the day?"

Someone said, "Who can suffer more than God, who has been to every funeral all through this world's existence?"

Who can suffer more than God, whose heart got deeply broken when Lucifer and his angels rebelled against Him who created all the angels to worship Him?"

Who can suffer more than God, who created this world so perfect with a perfect man and a perfect woman who broke His heart when they disobeyed God in a perfect Garden of Eden?

Who can say they have suffered more than God, whose heart was deeply broken when His only begotten son died on the cross to save the whole world from being lost in sin?

Who can suffer more than God, who we hurt every time we sin against Him?

A foolish person can make fun of people's sins, which deeply hurts God, suffered with His Son for the holy angels to feel the pain in heaven beyond the sun.

Many People Will Judge Me

Many people will judge me when they don't want to go through the things that I've been through. I say that Jesus Christ is my only judge.

Many people will judge me when they don't have the slightest clue about what my temptations and trials are. Jesus brought me through them all.

Many people will judge me many more times than a few when they don't want to walk in my shoes. My Lord and savior Jesus Christ walked in to save me from being lost in my sins.

Many people will judge me all through my life, when they wouldn't want to take on my illnesses and my grief. Jesus Christ took them on through the price He paid on the cross.

Many people will judge me with their jokes about me when they don't know how serious Jesus will keep His oath to me as if I was the only sinner He wants to save.

Many people will judge me for their reasons, even though they're not good reasons. They can't figure out the reason Jesus opens doors for me before and after I lay down to sleep.

Many people will judge me so deeply in their thoughts when they haven't seen Jesus lifting me up out of the deep pits of sin and bringing me this far. I will only be judged by Him.

Up in High Places

Some people have friends up in high places to get things done for them, and they embrace these high-placed friends.

Being up in high places is a joy for the rich, who especially have friends in high places each and every day.

I have a friend who is up in the highest place, like the bible says about heaven where my Lord and savior Jesus Christ is crowned the king of kings.

Jesus is my best friend, who looks down from heaven on me and gets things done for me.

In Him, I have a friend who is high up in the highest place that will forever be above presidents in the White House.

No other place can get higher than heaven, where Jesus is the everlasting truth. No liar will ever tarnish His holy name.

Many people have done wrong things in high places here on earth, where blame is like a sport to play.

In Him, I have a friend up in the highest place who gets good things done for me so many more times than a few.

Where is God?

Where is God when the hurricanes and tornadoes blow down anything that's in the way of their angry path?

God is there as He allows the hurricanes and tornadoes to have their way with us who can't question God, whom the storms will obey.

Where is God when wars kill so many people with their blood spilled all over the land?

God is there in His still, quiet voice ready to call the living to trust His will and do His will. When they die or get killed, God is there, even before they go to the grave. We must choose to believe in his Son Jesus Christ to be saved.

Where is God when our enemies come our way?

God is there to give us the strength to live for him like it's our last day to live, as if our enemies will kill us dead.

Where is God when church folks are not spiritually fed with all the truth in the bible?

God is there with his Son, who is the head of the church to put out His law in people's hearts.

Why Me?

Why me, who would be so lost in my sins if Jesus didn't save me from my sins before my life ends?

Why me who must suffer for Jesus' name's sake if I am a real, true Christian and being no fake?

Why me, who is so blessed to still be alive and doing God's will even after my heart is broken from losing some loved ones that are gone to the grave hopefully saved in Jesus Christ

Why me, who is no better than anyone else who Jesus loves to save and one day take with Him to heaven above this old sinful world that has so many questions not being answered.

Why me, who can't see what Jesus sets before me each and every day, but I have the free will to choose to say why me.

Jesus is not through with me yet, and no one can tell me His plans for me.

Why me, who needs to be about living for Jesus without a doubt.

Jesus Can Give Us the Strength

Jesus can give us the strength to overcome our pain if we believe that He can without a doubt upon His holy name

Jesus can give us the strength to overcome our fears if we believe that He can day after day and year after year.

Jesus can give us the strength to overcome our unforgiveness if we believe that He can for those who hurt us to see that we hold no grudges to be set free.

Jesus can give us the strength to overcome our weaknesses if we believe He can make us strong over our flesh to get relieved from the lust of the world and from the pride of life.

Jesus can give us the strength to overcome our selfish ways \if we believe that He can like seeing the sun shining down its beautiful rays.

Jesus can give us the strength to overcome anything if we believe that He can to be like hearing the birds sing.

We Can Tailgate Our Own Life

We can tailgate our own life by spiritually driving on the bumper of our health that we should always love to take good care of for the Lord to fully use us for His glory in heaven above.

We can tailgate our own life by spiritually driving on the bumper of our soul that we can put in danger by not allowing the truth of God to set us free from that old lying devil who loves to drive on the bumper of our soul's salvation.

The Lord gives us the power to work out our own soul's salvation by using our free will choice to choose to love and obey Him.

We can tailgate our own life by spiritually driving on the bumper of our hearts that we can deny with motives and intentions to crash in sinning against the Lord.

Jesus will never tailgate our lives to stress us to get onboard with His salvation.

Jesus will always keep his distance to never tailgate our lives, even when we surely drive on the bumper of breaking his ten golden rules.

Pleasing You, My Lord

Pleasing You, my Lord, will clear my mind from the dark clouds of doubting You who are always on time to help me get through the uncertain days.

Pleasing You, my Lord Jesus, will give me strong roots of trusting Your ways that will never change on me on my good days and bad days.

My time belongs to You to please You, who shows mercy on me for not always making the right choices in my life.

You, my Lord, are long-suffering with me to come this far in my life to please You who loves to please my heart with Your love and with Your holy word that starts my day off for me.

I love and obey You, my Lord Jesus Christ, who I love to please the most every day in my life.

We Can Come So Close

We can come so close to an accident that every Christian knows that the Lord kept it from happening to us.

His miraculous protection blows our minds, especially when we can't protect ourselves like Jesus can. He protects you and me who can come so close to death on any day.

Those who will obey Jesus, who can give us another day to live, need to say thank you, Lord, for sparing my life to live to see this day.

We can come so close to not giving Jesus the glory and praise for all that he does for us.

We can come so close to not putting all or our trust in Jesus each and every day.

Every Christian must come so close to Jesus Christ, instead of pushing Him away from us and doing our own will.

Our love for Jesus is serious businesses; Jesus doesn't play.

From You, O Lord

Good doctors and good medicine are from You, O Lord, who blesses this world with more and more good nurses. They are all from You, O Lord.

My Lord Jesus Christ is so good all the time to everyone in this life.

Good people are from You, O Lord, no matter what race, creed or color they are here below Your heaven on high.

Good things are from You, My Lord Jesus Christ, the king of kings whose throne will never end before fallen men whose sins are not from You.

O Lord, You give us so many good days to choose to live our lives doing Your holy will.

That is from You, my Lord Jesus Christ.

On This Day in Time

If Jesus had waited to come to this world on this day in time, many religious leaders would reject Him in every way.

If Jesus had come to this world on this day in time to feed the hungry, cast out demons and heal the sick throughout the world, many religious leaders would get jealous.

If Jesus had come to this world on this day in time to tell us that He is the Son of God, many religious leaders would want Him thrown in jail, even though Jesus is so good to everyone.

God didn't make a mistake when He sent his Son into this world at the right time that is long gone under the sun.

Many religious leaders today are no different from the religious leaders in the bible who were so against Jesus Christ, who is still the light of the world today.

He is there to save every man, woman, boy and girl.

Jesus is coming back again in these last days of time, and many religious leaders are still rejecting Jesus as the true vine.

We Can Ill Life

We can ill life for doing our own thing when life will obey Jesus Christ the king of kings.

We can ill life for making bad choices when life will always choose to love Jesus Christ.

We can ill life for making this sinful world our home when Jesus is building us a heavenly mansion above the sky dome.

We can ill life for laying up our treasures in this world when nothing in this world can ever measure up to Jesus.

We can ill life for believing to be self-made when it's Jesus who brought us this far beyond our mistakes.

We can ill life for being self-righteous when only the blood of Jesus can cleanse us of our sins.

Wherever I Go

Wherever I go, my shadow will be with me to let me know that I am real to see.

Wherever I go, the sky will hover over me while being so high above the tallest trees.

Wherever I go, the ground will be below me as the ground lays down so still under my feet.

Wherever I go, the air will be with me to breathe it in and out of my nostrils so free.

Wherever I go, God will be with me if I have His holy spirit in me to be a Christian believing in His Son, Jesus Christ.

Wherever I go, my life won't cave in on me if I love and obey Jesus who has no sins.

Wherever I go, my walk with Jesus won't shake like an earthquake that I never experience and not because I have done good works upon the land.

Wherever I go, my destiny is in my hands whether I'm a wise or foolish man.

Life is a Pathway

Life is a pathway that the living take, day after day. Life is no mistake that the Lord can make.

Life is a pathway that the dead can't walk through, day after day. The living can talk to the Lord Jesus Christ, who is the life, the way and the truth.

Life is a pathway day after day that the living can choose to say and do things with the free will choice that the Lord will judge for us to be saved or lost.

Life is a pathway that the sun goes down on and rises up on for the living to know that the Lord has His hand on life to bless us if we live unto Him who was a sinless man on the pathway of life.

Jesus made this pathway for us to live.

The Best People to Be Around

The best people to be around are people who love Jesus day after day.

You and I need to be around people who love Jesus, who will bless our lives in so many ways.

The best people to be around are people who are saved in Jesus, who gave up His life to save us from our sins. Jesus rose from the grave to give us eternal life.

Jesus has gone down in history and He is no mystery to us today.

The best people to be around for you and me are people who love Him and obey Him, who sees every Christian.

We will go through some kind of storm in life for Jesus' name's sake, and Christians are always the best people to be around.

Grief Over a Loved One

Grief over a loved one is a painful experience to go through day after day, but Jesus can strengthen you and me to make it through the loss of our loved ones.

Grief is nothing new under the sun, where many people grieve over a mother, father, husband, wife, sister, son, daughter, brother or friend.

Jesus loves and gives his saving grace to those grieving and lets us know that we can face up to the lost of our loved ones who we hope are saved in Jesus Christ.

He rose from the grave to give you and me and our loved ones eternal life when He comes back again.

We will grieve only for a moment in this world that will one day pass away with grief and pain that Jesus will wipe away like the ground drying up after the rain.

A Ram in the Bush

The Lord always has a ram in the bush for his children.

We can trust the Lord to push forward in blessing us with something better for our good.

Our Lord Jesus Christ always has a ram in the bush that will show you and me that the Lord is always on time to encourage us to wait on Him who is always so divine.

The Lord gives us a spiritual ram in the bush that we will find to be a blessing.

We can't give up when the Lord shows us what He can do for us in this world where nothing is promised to us except the Lord's promises.

We can always trust the Lord to give us a ram in the bush on His holy ground that has many spiritual rams.

This day, Jesus wants us to put Him first on our list of things.

Jesus always follows through for me and you, so we can know what He will always do.

When There is Nothing Left

When there is nothing left for us to say, Jesus always has something to say in His holy word day after day.

When there is nothing left to do, Jesus can always do something for us if we get down on our knees and pray to Him, he will do good things for us according to His will.

When there is nothing left to say and nothing to do, Jesus is always there for you and me to listen to what He has to say and to see what He can do for us, even when we run out of words and things to say and do.

We can't imagine and never see all that Jesus has for us. He always has something left for you and me to say and do when we make it to heaven above, where there is always something to say and do in God's love.

When I Don't See My Way Through

When I don't see my way through my burdens, You, my Lord, clear my pathway so I can walk through.

When I don't see my way through my trials, You, my Lord, give me the strength to get through them and do Your holy will.

When I don't see my way through my life, You, my Lord, open up my eyes so I can see the price You paid for me to live my life unto You day after day.

When I don't see my way through this world, You, my Lord, show me the way to your holy word that will set me free from the world's selfishness that loves to oppress me and make me not do Your will that is so right all the time.

When I don't see my way through my heart, You, my Lord, will shine Your light all through my heart so I can love and obey You who gives the sun its beautiful rays to shine all around me when I don't see my way through the day.

Blow Our Minds

No one can blow our minds like Jesus Christ, our Lord.

He can blow our minds so much more than money and luck, which can never lift us up like Jesus, who we can always trust to blow our minds.

We know that He can do anything but fail us.

We don't have a clue how Jesus can blow our minds like He blew his disciples' minds when he healed the sick, raised the dead, cast out demons, and fed the hungry.

Jesus led them to repent of their sins and follow Him.

He is the head of the church and will always blow our minds and we are glad to worship Him and give Him the glory and praise.

Jesus can blow our minds and make us so amazed about what He can do for us, no mater what anyone says.

Heaven is So High

Heaven is so high because of God, who lives in heaven above me and you.

Our best dreams can't come close to heaven above. It is so high in God's everlasting love that fills up the heavens.

The angels truly know forever and ever that they will worship God so pure in their hearts.

Heaven is so high above the earth where mortal men can lie, but God cannot lie.

He gave us His only begotten son, who came from heaven above so very long ago to save us from our sins.

Our sins can never enter into heaven that is so high above this fallen world.

Heaven is the eternity that is waiting on me and you.

Are Actions Always True?

Are actions always true, when we may do something good for the wrong reasons?

We can never do something bad for a good reason. That won't work in the presence of the Lord.

We can do something good for the wrong reason. That would make our actions not be true.

Season in and season out of the summer, fall, winter and spring, pure actions are always true and bring us good and well in our lives.

Our choices will lead our actions to be good or bad so real.

Many people can go through the motions of and have no true faith in the Lord Jesus Christ, whose hands and feet were always true in actions because His heart was always true in loving God.

When Has Love Ever Hurt Anyone?

When has love ever hurt anyone?

Love will never hurt our hearts under the sun.

When has love ever hurt anyone?

Who can say that love is bad no matter where we are from?

Love has never hurt anyone.

Sorrow and abandonment can hurt us, who always need to follow the Lord Jesus Christ. He loves us all the time.

Jesus will never hurt us. We can always find love in Him because He will never hurt anyone.

Jesus has no lies and no deception in Him. He has no sins and will never fall short of love.

Jesus is a great and perfect friend to us all.

We will never be hurt by love that God gives to all men.

Will Put Their Trust In

Many people will put their trust in what they say, even though that may only be hot air that will get cold.

Jesus is the way to trust beyond words every day.

Many people will put their trust in what they know and how they feel.

Jesus knows all things for us to trust in Him from day to day.

Our chances are dim and slim if we put our trust in the visible things that we see.

We don't see Jesus but we can trust Him to be there.

Many people will put their trust in what they do, but that can breed mistakes.

Jesus is a friend we can always trust to lead us to what we need.

Many people will put their trust in things that are lethal.

Put your trust in Jesus and he will lead you to life eternal.

Today

Be happy about what you can do today for the Lord, who is a today Lord and savior who will save you and me from our sins.

Today, you and I can choose to love our neighbors. We can help them to see that Jesus is real in us.

Today can only give us today, not yesterday and not tomorrow. Tomorrow is like a question mark waiting for an answer.

Today is from the Lord for us to know that we can give a helping hand to those in need of the Lord who wants us to be thankful unto him.

Today, life owes nothing to you and me, but we owe our lives to Jesus Christ today.

Yesterday is gone away and tomorrow can be far away, especially if we are sick today and may not get well before tomorrow.

Today may be all that we have to search and find the Lord, who we need today to get onboard and get our salvation reward.

Some Questions Will Never be Answered

Some questions will never be answered in this world so far away and below the heavenly gates of everlasting pearls.

Some questions will never be answered, like who created God or did God create Himself? We don't know the answers.

It's very odd to think we could figure out where God came from, when our minds are too small to imagine God being forever beyond our time here on earth.

Some questions will never be answered, like how big is God, how can He be everywhere in the day and night, and how does God live forever beyond this sinful world?

Some questions will never be answered, like did anyone exist before God? We will never know.

What we do know is that God exists through our faith in Him, even though we've never seen Him.

In our faith, we know that God will answer our prayers.

Some questions will never be answered under the sun, where we didn't create ourselves to exist without God who's work never goes undone.

Nobody Can Take Away

Nobody can take away what you believe. Only you can choose or not choose to give up your beliefs.

Nobody can take away your choice. You can make your choice without your voice being heard.

Nobody can take away your love, but you can take that away from yourself and treat yourself badly.

Nobody can take away your thoughts, even though you might not see the mistakes of your bad thoughts.

Nobody can take away what's in your heart. Your heart is filled with what you put in it and you should not lend out what you owe to your heart.

Nobody can take away your soul salvation and nobody can take away your destiny today or tomorrow.

Nobody can take away your hope and trust in Jesus Christ, who died and rose from the dust of the earth.

Life Can Make Us or Break Us

Many people will say that life is what you make it.

Life can make us change our ways for than a little bit.

Life can break us down to be humble unto the Lord, who gives us life to live until Him.

He is before life and after life. He makes us aware of who we are.

Life can break us to be like a tale being told that the Lord always knows so very well.

He is the author of the life we live every day.

Life can make us free to choose to give God the glory and the praise.

Life can break us to feel sorrow and grief until we lick the dust.

But we can live forever in Jesus Christ, who will come back again to give us eternal life if we are saved in this life.

Life can't make or break our free will that God gave to us so we can choose who we will serve today.

We Were Born to Serve

We were born to serve the Lord with our whole heart. Jesus wants that from us day after day.

We should start each day with serving the Lord.

We were born to also serve one another with our gifts and talents wherever we go.

We must serve with good deeds, love people and serve their needs in Jesus's holy and precious name.

Jesus will bless our service work and we will have no blame.

We were born to especially serve the Lord, and be joyful about serving one another and anyone who has needs.

We all fall short of God's glory in one way or another, but we were born to serve every day.

Community service is of the Lord who loves for us to help our neighbors more and more.

Rotating on Its Axis

We can't stop life from rotating on its axis of change.

Life will take us through some changes so plain and simple.

The Lord wants to renew our lives unto Him.

You and I can't stop life from rotating on its axis of uncertainty that breathes hot air on us every day that God loves us in our lifetime that is short and can leave us at any time.

We can't stop life from rotating on its axis of wondering what kind of life we will live.

Hopefully we will live our lives unto Jesus Christ, who gives life the power to rotate on its axis for you and me to live doing His Will.

Life can surely rotate on its axis of the Lord being in charge of life to make our presence known before Him.

Yesterday, today and tomorrow, life will rotate on its axis of showing us the way to Jesus in a world that has gone astray from the Lord God when only a few will do what the Lord says.

Everybody in Church

Everybody in church will not talk right, do right and will not dress right in the precious eyesight of God.

He loves us all, even if our hearts are not right with Him who loves us for who we are.

Everybody in church will be held accountable for their own sins. You and I are guilty of our sins before God, who gave us His only begotten son to die for our sins on the cross where you and I should have hung in guilt and shame.

Everybody in church has a name that is like filthy rags before God, who's son Jesus Christ is above every name.

Jesus can renew everyone's life in the church, but everybody is not like Jesus who is holy and righteous around the clock.

Love to Talk About

We live in a world where many people love to talk about other people

They love to talk about what people do, as if there is no creator God who made people to serve Him.

God is the life-giver and the only superb God over all people every day.

Many people in the church love to talk about people's sins, as if they don't have any sins of their own to confess and repent of unto the Lord Jesus Christ.

Jesus will test you and me to talk about Him who we should love to always talk about.

He is merciful and good, and that's what we should be talking about.

We can talk about people and get no real fulfillment to have inner peace upon the land.

The Beginning

We need to go back to the beginning of our baby walk with the Lord that went hand in hand with our baby talk about the Lord, who gave us a beginning.

It was so good for us to start our Christian journey with a beautiful glow of surrendering our hearts unto the Lord Jesus Christ who brought us this far in our renewed Christian life.

We experience spiritual growth in His grace and truth. That wasn't with us in the beginning.

We sat down at Jesus' banquet table when we were babies, and we ate spiritual baby food with Him to begin our walk with our best friend who is the beginning and end of our talk and walk — our Lord.

He knows how to take us back to the beginning without a doubt.

He lets us know that we didn't bring ourselves this far to continue to follow the bright and morning star.

The Path of the World

The path of the world is a pathway to a dead end below the path to heaven beyond the sun where no sin exists.

This world is filled with destruction here and there.

The path of the world is full of selfishness and no love.

Jesus Christ, our Lord, has a path of eternal life for you and me to walk down, if we love him above this world that will do us so wrong sooner or later for trusting in temporary things more than Jesus Christ, who is the king of kings and lord of lords.

The path of the world will bring us to a dead end of being lost and never going to heaven that our eyes have never seen.

Only Imaginary

Our moment in time is only imaginary, compared to God who is a real, eternal presence.

He will never, ever part from who He is beyond our presence that is short to be like a tale being told compared to God who is eternal.

Our life on earth is only imaginary compared to God, who lives forever and ever and can be anywhere at the same time.

Everything is only real through God.

We can't imagine all that He can do under and beyond the great blue sky, which is only imaginary compared to God.

No one is more real than God, who proves that in Jesus.

Only a food wouldn't see who God sent from heaven to pay our price that was not imaginary to the devil, who knows that Jesus is real and gives us eternal life.

If We Question the Lord

If we question the Lord, we must be prepared to get our answer and it might not be something we like to hear.

All things beyond our questions prove we have little faith in Him who will never have a need to question you and me about anything.

He already knows more about everything than we will ever know about anything.

Asking questions will prove that we don't know all the answers in this world where little children can ask some hard questions that many parents can't answer.

The Lord has all the right answers to all our questions and the bible can answer in the Lord's will, no matter where we live.

We may or may not like the answers from the Lord, who can ask us a question that we might not be able to handle upon this sinful land.

Life is Full

Life is full of twists and turns. We don't know what will happen next in this complex world that is so unpredictable every day.

Life is full of crimes, non-stop around the clock.

When the time on our biological clocks is unknown, we don't know how long we will live to hopefully see Jesus Christ coming back again on the clouds of glory.

Life is full of tales being told in a story written in many books that have no better truth than the bible.

The bible tells us about the fallen man and the bread of life being full of God's love in his son, Jesus Christ, who gave us salvation so we can one day be with him beyond this world.

Heaven is full of eternal life in Jesus Christ, who overcame this world of sin for you and me to be full of living our lives unto Him through thick and thin.

Our Prayer Guard

We need to keep our prayer guard up every day.

We need to pray to Jesus Christ our only way to enteral life in heaven above this world.

We will get weak in our flesh without prayer to set us free from trusting what we see that can't give us strength to overcome this world that will get the best of us if we don't keep our prayer guard up.

We can't afford to lay it down in our hearts and need to pray sincerely to God.

He gives us a prayer guard against the unknown that would crush our hope and dreams if we didn't trust Jesus to always pray to him.

He rose from the dust of the earth for us to never lay our prayer guard down because Jesus is alive to answer our prayers right now.

God is Ongoing and Non-Stop

God is ongoing and non-stop in what he does to be always good and right beyond the endless universe.

He watches our days and numbers them for us to stop living, but God goes on and on, non-stop.

The works of men will depart through time that will stop one day at the end of this world.

Only God is ongoing and non-stop beyond sin that God will someday put a stop to.

Sin wishes that it was non-stop, but it only seems that way for us.

We can't forget that we live in a sinful world that is temporary.

God is ongoing and non-stop all through the ongoing eternity.

God will stop by our hearts with His ongoing and non-stop love.

We can stop loving god, but that will cause us to miss out on an ongoing and non-stop heavenly bliss.

The Last

We don't know when we will think our last thought, which will hopefully be to exhort the Lord.

Life is too short for us and we don't know when we will say our last word in the land of the living.

Our days are going by fast to the end of our lives, and we don't know if we'll live another day.

We don't know the last thing we will do before we lay down our heads to sleep and maybe never wake up to say another word or do another thing again.

While we are alive today, we should live our lives giving Jesus Christ our hearts, minds and souls, as if it was our last day to live in the last days of this world that is no friend to us.

We can't wait to the last hour to repent of our sins and come to Jesus to lend us more time before the end.

I Can Always be Myself

I can always be myself when I talk to you, O Lord.

I can get everything out in the open with You and avoid any pretense.

I can always pour out all of my heart to You, my Lord Jesus.

You will never cause me to shut down my feelings and you fully understand me more than anyone else.

I can always be myself with you in the land of the living.

I can't always be myself with anyone else.

No one else but You will help me bear my burdens and love me when I'm always myself.

With your encouragement and strength, I can hold on and do Your will.

I can always be myself with You, O Lord, who loves me so faithfully and true.

I know you've been in my shoes that I have worn out all the way through.

Cover Up

We wear clothes to cover up our nakedness that some people love to show to anyone, no matter where they are.

Many people will cover up their body parts really well because they believe that it's the right thing to do to show respect for ourselves and others.

Covering up our sins and not confessing them is the wrong thing to do before the Lord around the clock.

We can't cover up our spiritual nakedness before the Lord, no matter how well we are covered up in our clothes that we can wear so confidently wherever we go from day to day.

Our sins are so naked before the Lord, and we can confess and repent them unto the Lord, who will cover our souls in His righteousness.

Gods love covers up our naked life choices from our naked hearts if we are right with Him.

Jesus can clothe us in His mercy and grace every day.

It Was My Cross

It wasn't your cross, O Lord, that you carried and died on for me to be saved in You; it was my cross.

You know that I couldn't bear all of my sins that I deserve to die for, so you cared to do Your heavenly Father's will and become all of my sins on the cross.

It was my cross that you carried, my flaws of sin that you bore in my place, Lord Jesus Christ.

You truly gave up Your life on my cross that was meant for me. You saved me when I couldn't save myself.

You, O Lord, proved Yourself on the cross that I couldn't bear to hang on and deserved to die on.

Surely only You, Lord Jesus Christ, were all about taking on my cross and taking my place. You saved me from my sins that you became on the cross.

You gave me grace when you rose from the grave.

What Does it Add Up To?

What does it all add up to in your life if you subtract Jesus Christ from your life and act like you can do it all on your own?

Sooner or later you'll fail and everything you've done will add up to nothing good for your soul.

What does it all add up to if you go astray from Jesus, who knows how to add up eternal life for your soul?

The devil is always bad and adds up your sins that only Jesus can subtract and take away if you and I confess and repent every day.

If you don't obey and confess to Jesus, your life will add up to zero.

If we subtract Jesus from our lives, hell will surely be our destination.

In Simple Ways

The Lord can show His faithfulness to us in simple ways that we can see so we can trust Him to do what he says.

The Lord can show us His power in simple ways so we know that He can heal our hearts and make us strong enough to go on loving Him day after day.

For as long as we live, the Lord can hold our hands and show us His goodness in simple ways so we can understand, repent and turn away from our sins.

The Lord can show us on any day the simple things we need to do to earn His forgiveness upon our souls.

He can show us His love in simple ways, like a beautiful flower getting our attention.

We Can Live in Fantasy in the Church

We can live in fantasy in the church if we believe that we can separate the wheat from the tares and judge a man by the deeds of his hands.

We can live in fantasy in the church if we believe that we have no sins to confess and repent of unto the Lord Jesus Christ, who is the head of the church and it is no fantasy in our lives.

The people of the world believe that Jesus is a fantasy that we true Christians believe in Jesus to be real in the church.

If we believe that our works can save our souls, then we are living in a fantasy in the church that God will judge first.

The unrighteous lives in sin that is very real to our lives and will give us death that is no fantasy.

You and I can live in fantasy in the church if we believe that we can cast our own sins out to the bottom of the deepest sea.

A Dream to Hold Onto

Only a few out of many have found their true love.

Many are dreaming about finding their true love to sparkle like the stars on a clear night.

Dreaming about finding true love is a dream to hold onto in a world of many broken dreams that seem so cold and cruel to good loving people.

Those who long for their dream to come true one day should know that a true soul mate is from the Lord, who makes dreams come true on time and not late.

There are people who have found their true loves early in life because of the Lord making it be so right.

The best dream to hold onto is going to heaven above where love never ends in Jesus Christ, the greatest true love of all souls that he can save from being lost in sin.

The Greatest

The devil wanted to be the greatest.

God brought him down to the smallest that he deserves all around the world.

The Lord will bring proud people down so they will know that He is worthy to be praised above all things.

The devil can't say and do anything about it.

Evil people will live their days wanting to be like God and be the greatest.

God is all-wise and above fools who believe they are self-made and great in their own eyes. They're just earning themselves early graves.

Death is everyone's fate, and no one can be great in this game.

Jesus Christ is the greatest to give us life another day because he paid the greatest price to save every soul who believes in Him.

He is the greatest provider in our spiritual eyesight.

Will Sooner or Later Show and Tell

When motives and intentions are not good, it will sooner or later show and tell in words and in actions for us to know that everyone doesn't mean you and me good and well.

There is a hidden agenda.

Loving people will show and tell their true motives and true intentions.

Anyone can choose to believe in Jesus Christ with the free will choice that you and I have every day to do one another good and not evil.

What we do to others will sooner or later come back to us in ways that we don't even realize.

The Lord knows about our sins that we can't afford to not confess and repent of.

We can't believe that our sins won't show and tell on us sooner or later.

We can't be deceived that this will be all right with the Lord.

We are bad off to grieve the Holy Ghost who will sooner or later show and tell on lost souls.

To Live Another Day

Who am I to live another day when a good person will die today? I don't know why the Lord allows this.

Jesus allowed me to live another day that a little child won't see, even though I may stray away from the Lord in some kind of way.

A God-fearing person will die today, saved from their sins to sleep among the righteous dead.

I am alive another day that the Lord let me live to call out His name on high this day.

I am no better than anyone else in Jesus' eyes.

Many people breathed their last breath yesterday and won't live another day, even though Jesus allowed me to live to do His holy will.

I may not live to see the tomorrow that the Lord will give to many other people who do not do His holy will that is forever real yesterday, today and tomorrow.

Jesus gives nobody a bad deal and won't let them die without a fair chance to be saved in God's grace.

If We are Christians

If we are Christians, we won't find any joy in doing something wrong any time of the day or night.

If we are Christians, we won't find peace in doing something wrong from the start of the day to the end of the day.

Our hearts should be filled with Jesus Christ.

If we are Christians, we won't find freedom in doing something wrong and becoming a slave to sin. Sin will always see no wrong in doing something wrong.

For as long as we shall live, we will hopefully be Christians doing God's holy will. It is always right to do in a world of many wrongdoings every day.

If we are Christians, we won't find love in doing something wrong that is selfishness under heaven above.

Are We Ready

Are we ready to love people joining our church with some bad attitudes that just won't work out for our good?

Jesus Christ had to choose twelve disciples who were not perfect from head to toe, day to day.

We should be ready to accept people for who they are if we love Jesus as we go through our testing times in the church of Jesus Christ.

He knows if we are ready to give up our lives for His holy name's sake that has no blemish or blame.

Jesus is always ready to save the lost who believe in his name.

We may not be ready to see Jesus fill up the church with real people who want to do God's will.

Be ready for Jesus to move you and me out of their way if we are not ready to love and obey Jesus with all of our hearts.

Will Never be Satisfied with Anything

If we don't live for Jesus, we will never be satisfied with anything.

We will want more of everything that we think will satisfy us.

The only way that will happen is if we love and obey Jesus. Then, we'll be satisfied with Him day after day.

We won't be satisfied with anything if we don't glorify Jesus as the king of kings and lord of lords in our lives.

You and I won't be satisfied with anything if we don't accept Jesus who can set us free with the truth of His word. It can satisfy our souls with peace.

We will never be satisfied with anything from our heads to our feet if we don't trust Jesus to work out our problems and meet us where we are in our hearts.

Jesus can cleanse us of our sins through the blood He shed for us to win the victory and be satisfied in doing God's will.

God's will is beyond anything else that has no real, true satisfaction under the sun.

Pain Can Make Us Stronger

Pain can make us stronger in the Lord whether it's physical or emotional pain.

It can make us do better in life and be a blessing to others who may feel some pain in their bodies and their hearts, and those who might have got a bad deal in life.

Jesus Christ, our Lord and savior, gives His love to you and me regardless of the pain we feel.

We can still glorify Jesus' holy name in our pain, even if it comes upon us unexpectedly.

Pain can make us stronger in the Lord Jesus Christ who we can always trust to take our pain away if it's in His will to relieve us of that pain.

We can truly believe that in time He will take us beyond our pain and grief.

Not Keeping Watch

Many church folks are not keeping watch for Jesus coming back one day soon for His children who he loves to be saved in Him.

It's not the time to spiritually sleep away into worldly things under the sunshine.

This world has nothing to offer but eternal death in the end, and that watch will be over.

We must deny self today to pick up our cross and follow Jesus Christ.

He keeps a watch over our lives day after day, even though many church folks stray away from keeping watch for Him.

They're not watching what the bible says about falling spiritually asleep in putting trust in this world that will one day pass away with all of its sins.

Is Not Alone

The earth is not alone; it has the sun to keep it company in the universe, and the stars keep the moon company all night long.

The Lord will never leave us alone in this world of sin that is everywhere.

The sky is not alone; it has the clouds to keep it company up in the sky.

Jesus Christ, our Lord, will not leave us alone in this life and in the eternal life to come to us if we are saved in Jesus.

He keeps us company in God's amazing grace that won't leave us alone for as long as we live on the face of the earth.

Jesus won't leave you and me alone, even if we feel so alone in our homes.

Many People in Church

Many people in church will be lost for only loving certain people who have no voice in heaven to speak before God or make our appeals in the presence of God. Only Jesus Christ can do that so real.

Many church folks will be lost because of their pride and trying to make themselves look good. They aren't humble in the eyes of the Lord. He knows that everybody in the church will not be saved.

Many people in church will be lost in their works that can't save you and me, no matter how good those works are. They don't mean that Jesus lives in our hearts twenty-four hours around the clock.

Many people in church will be lost for not being in Jesus' true flock.

It Would Be Great to See

It would be great to see all of my loved ones being saved in Jesus Christ as the sun rises and as the sun sets over this world.

It would be great to see the church being filled with saved people who have been set free from living in sin to love the Lord Jesus Christ.

It would be great to see my loved ones living a Christian life to love and obey Jesus, who has given us His ten golden rules as a great thing for all men to keep, which would be a great thing to see.

Living in sin is a bad thing for Jesus to see because he gave up His life on the cross to pay our price and save us from our sins.

It would be great to see it all disappear one day, when Jesus comes back again.

God Made Things

God made things to be eternal.

Man makes things that can burn in an inferno.

God makes things that will never fade away.

Man makes things that can erode and rust every day.

God made things that will last to the end.

Man makes things that can break down and bend out of shape.

God made things that will cause the birds to sing praises unto Him whose Son is the king of kings.

Man makes things that can bring on disappointments that can sting us like a bee, which doesn't feel good at all.

God made things that will never fall into pieces.

Man makes things that can do us all harm, great and small.

If It's Not One Thing, It's Another

If it's not one thing, it's another, because we don't always see things coming our way.

Jesus Christ, our Lord, is so good to us to move things out of our way in his time that flows through.

We don't always know what's going on with one thing or another, even when it can be a burden to you and me.

Jesus will never burden us with what He brings our way. It will strengthen us and make us hold tight to Him day after day.

You and I will make choices to come by our way whether they are right or wrong for one thing or another.

Jesus will always see what choices we should make.

We can sting ourselves with bad choices that can cause one thing to become another thing without a pause.

Jesus can be for us regardless of our sinful flaws.

It Would be Wrong

It would be wrong if everybody loved me, many would dislike me if they see me living a Christian life and believing in Jesus Christ.

It would be wrong if everybody disliked me for living a life of obedience unto the Lord. But, there are also righteous people who love me for being a Christian who loves Jesus and obeys His ten golden rules.

Not everyone will obey Jesus, because they don't love Him.

I can always pray for everybody who doesn't know Him.

It would be wrong if everybody was against me who God is so good to. He would make my enemies make peace with me.

He finds favor with me from the greatest to the least of my problems.

Jesus can always work out my problems from my head to my feet.

We Will Never Run Out of Needs

We will never run out of needs in this world of more needs where people want things they don't need, especially from the Lord.

The Lord will supply all of our true needs day after day.

We will never run out of needs that we can surely see, especially among the poor. They never run out of needing this and needing that, day after day.

We can afford to miss out on some of our wants for things that the Lord is not concerned about.

We especially need the Lord, who is always right about knowing what our needs are every day and every night that we will never run out of needs.

Our wants can run out, because the Lord will never put our wants above our true needs, without a doubt.

Our needs will outweigh our wants to the Lord, He will see that we get everything we truly need.

Like a Mystery

Not knowing what tomorrow will bring is like a mystery.

The dark covers the sky, bringing in the night like a mystery in our eyesight that has the light of vision to know that God made it so right for us to see.

We don't get to see the unknown. It's like a mystery to us, who God will never leave along for loving Him.

God's love for us is like a mystery that we can never solve.

We don't really see why God loves sinners like us.

Us still being here is like a mystery that follows us to the grave.

Many people don't live to see another day, and that is like a mystery to us who don't know when we will lick the dust.

The Heart Will Speak Actions

The heart will speak actions when words can speak hot air that can leak like air leaking from a tire that goes flat.

The heart will speak actions when words can speak sweet nothings from the start to the end of the day.

Actions are more true than words that can speak lies all through the day and night.

The heart will speak actions to you and me, showing the real person in our actions that speak so true about what's in our hearts.

We don't always know everything without a doubt, but God knows what our hearts will say before we say one word.

The heart will speak actions every day, but words can speak only cheap talk.

The heart will speak actions that will walk the walk no matter where we live.

Make a Spiritual Investment

Money can be in my hands today and be out of my hands today, because money will come and go with wings and fly away.

Spiritual things will last forever beyond our years of doing the Lord's will in season and out of season with no fear of running out like money in our hands.

We can use some money to make a spiritual investment and dedicate it unto the Lord, who will bless our hands to hold on to spiritual things to uplift His holy name.

Spending money on the wrong things can leave us feeling so empty because we can't put our trust in money, which can bring trouble our way if we love money more than the Lord.

He can set our hands free from investing in temporary things that can burden you and me.

Living a Mountain Life

Living a mountain life is a high life in living unto the things in this world that are high up, like a mountain for many singers to sing songs about in this world.

Living a mountain life is for those who enjoy the high life.

Jesus Christ lived a valley life here on earth.

He met people where they were in their needs, while the Pharisees here and there were living a mountain life.

They believed they were high up above Jesus in their deceitful ways, but Jesus saw what they were doing.

Jesus is the mountain of eternal life so high up above.

This life will one day go down in the valley of passing away from this world.

Jesus will make the world new with mountains of his blessings.

Jesus will fill every Christian life with a mountain of eternal zeal for the Lord on His holy mountain beyond the universal hills.

Doing Right by You, O Lord

Doing right by You, O Lord, I will never get burdened or ever feel bad.

Doing right by You, O Lord, will get me through the day.

I would be so lost if I sin against You, even though I'm aware of it being a sin. The choices I make do you so wrong, O Lord.

I want to do right by You and not live in the devil's lies that have nothing right in them for me to live by.

Doing right by You, O Lord, is right for me and the only way I can be blessed by You, who will always do me right no matter what I go through.

Don't Always Have to Let Others Know

You don't always have to let others know what good you have done so well.

The Lord foresees and sees if your heart is pure in doing good deeds that are always good for you and me to do unto the Lord.

He will lead and direct you and me to help our fellow man in his time of need.

You and I don't always know the Lord's purpose in our lives under the sunshine.

You and I don't always have to let others know that we are filled with the holy ghost, but they will surely see.

We can do something good for them so we can be a witness of Jesus, who didn't always want others to know that he healed people to fulfill God's will.

Strange Things Are Happening

So many strange things are happening in this world that will one day end with all of its sins.

There is a good strange thing that is happening to all the saints who are doing God's holy will.

We are strangers passing through this sinful world of so many bad strange things that can shock us from our head to our toes.

Jesus knows all the strange things and will truly protect you and me wherever we go.

Sin can cause strange things to happen and lets us see that time is short in this world.

We are not free from strange things going on.

You and I are strangers for being a Christian and knowing the true living God who will do a strange thing when he destroys this world one day.

Will Not Last Forever

O Lord, You will not let sickness and disease last for ever.

You will one day put it all at ease.

O Lord, You will not let heartache and grief last forever.

All who choose to believe in you will be saved into a new heaven and new earth.

There won't be any more sin in the land one day when Jesus comes back again. Jesus will not let pride and death last forever.

You are the breath of life to give eternal life to all who are born again in You.

You will cast death away under the stars one day.

You will come back again to last forever beyond this present time that will pass away at Your command, O Lord, for eternity to be glad.

Nobody is Left Out

Nobody is left out of God's love that we all can get from heaven above.

Nobody is left out of God's truth that is for all to live by and be made brand new in Jesus Christ who can save me and you.

Nobody is left out of God's salvation; it's given to every generation.

Nobody is left out of God's grace except the devil and his fallen angels. They are doomed to face God's judgment in the lake of fire and brimstone.

Wicked people will also go there for claiming to own all that God loans them.

We all were created to do God's will in the winter, spring, summer and fall.

We Can Always be Sure

We can always be sure about Jesus Christ, who will always surely renew our lives if we confess and repent of our sins.

We can always be sure about Jesus being our best friend from day to day.

We can't always be sure about what we will do and say. We may be out of touch with Jesus if we don't love and obey Him, who we can always be sure about.

Jesus will always do what he says he will do day after day.

You and I can always be sure about Jesus, who can surely cure our sin-sick souls and save us from being lost if we surely make Jesus our first choice.

Jesus Came From Eternity

Jesus came from eternity to a temporary world that reaps perilous times for every man, woman, boy and girl who needs to love and obey Jesus Christ.

He came from eternity to live a sinless life doing his heavenly Father's holy will to save sinners from being lost in our sins before we go to the grave.

Jesus came from God and went back to God, who is eternal along with his Son, Jesus, and the Holy Spirit.

God the father, the son and the Holy Spirit are one in eternity and will never come to an end beyond the sun.

This is where Jesus came from to save sinners from being lost.

God gives everyone a free will choice up in heaven and here on earth.

Jesus Cares About

That old devil doesn't care about what he put in our minds that makes us think evil thoughts that aren't divine.

Jesus cares about putting good thoughts in our minds all the time.

The devil doesn't care about what he put on our tongues that makes us say evil words that are wrong to say.

Jesus cares about putting good words on our tongues to bless people like He would always do with His holy word.

That old devil doesn't care about what he put in our hearts so that evil deeds come out and spread like a forest fire.

Jesus Christ cares about giving us a pure heart to do good deeds in life.

The devil doesn't care about good deeds because he loves to make strife and do evil.

I Can Call You Up

I can call you up any time, O Lord, and you will answer me who needs You.

No one else will always answer my call and talk to me.

I can always trust you, O Lord, to talk about anything and anyone who You truly know each and every day.

I can call you up, O Lord, who is up in heaven on high and sees all that I do before I do it.

Life's disappointments can surely get me down, but I can call you up, O Lord, and You will lift me up, as you talk to me so kind and real.

I can call you up any time, and get filled with Your holy ghost to do Your holy will.

I Would Rather Be

I would rather be alone and doing the Lord's will than keeping company with anyone who is not doing the Lord's will and getting filled with the devil.

I would rather suffer for doing the Lord's will than suffer for doing evil against the Lord, who hates selfishness.

Selfishness will cause us to fall into sin that can bring sorrow and death unto us all.

The Lord loves us and wants to save us from being lost.

I would rather be persecuted than live in sin that will fill my life with darkness and make me lost in the end.

I would rather be saved in the Lord Jesus Christ than go to hell because of not choosing to live right unto the Lord, who gives me life.

The Light Within Me

The light within me is Jesus Christ, who shines brighter than the sun all the time.

His light of love shines within me and gives me joy and peace that I can never get enough of day after day.

The light within me is Jesus for all the world to see shining within me.

The sun goes down and loses its light, but Jesus's light shines all around me, night and day.

Only Jesus Christ can make that light shine all around me every day and every night of my life.

I know that Jesus Christ paid the price for that light that shines within me.

I Will Live Again

When I die in Your holy name, O Lord, I will live again when You come back again in the sky where You, Lord Jesus, will raise me up from the grave because I am saved in You, O Lord.

You gave up Your life for me on the cross, and You rose from the grave for me to live again.

I love and worship You forever and ever all through eternal life.

I will live again without sin because of You, Lord Jesus, my best friend who let me live again in His holy name.

You will have no blemish and no blame wherever I go throughout the new heaven and new earth, where I will live again in You, O Lord, who loved me first.

As I Get Older

As I get older and draw closer to the grave, I want to draw closer to Jesus, who can save me and raise me up from the grave.

As I age, I don't have a lot of time left to be living in sin and wasting my life away by doing my own thing as if it's a good thing to do.

As I get older and have many dreams throughout the night, I dream that Jesus Christ is with me because I'm drawing closer to him.

Jesus sees and foresees my life and daily choices that I need to make right in doing His will.

As I get older my neighbors need to see Jesus living in me.

Before I go to the grave, I want to draw closer to Jesus under the sign of the rainbow.

The Lord Will Do Us Good

The Lord will do us good a lot more than we can ever do for ourselves.

The Lord will do us good in ways that we don't see until He reveals it to us.

We don't always do ourselves any good. We reap bad things that we bring on ourselves from our head to our feet.

The Lord will do us good even in our sleep. He will give us good dreams in the night under the beautiful white full moonlight.

The Lord will do us good, even if we know to do right and don't do it in his holy eyesight.

We need to repent of our sins and do the Lord good, because he loves both me and you.

I May Not

I may not have all the knowledge but I just want to be with You, O Lord, when you come back again through the universe.

I may not know all the bible truth about You, O Lord, who I want to be saved in.

I may not know all of my sins that You, my Lord Jesus, can forgive me for if I confess and repent before You, my Lord.

You know all things seen and unseen, but I may not know anything about my own heart.

It can deceive me, which You, O Lord, surely know.

You can set me free from what I may not know and can't see.

All that You see, O Lord, is for me to bow down on my knees before You, O Lord.

The True Joy About Life

The true joy about life is that I can pray and talk to You, O Lord, each and every day.

The true joy about life is that I can live my life unto You, O Lord, before my fellow man who won't find any other true joy in life like they would find in You, my Lord Jesus Christ.

You give me true joy, no matter what I go through in my life.

No one else can fill my life like my Lord, Jesus Christ.

The true joy that anyone can get is loving and obeying You, from day to day.

No one else can give me true joy like you, Lord Jesus. That, I can truly see.

Wherever Life Takes Me

Wherever life takes me, O Lord, I want to do Your holy will.

As I go through this life that can take me to places I don't know, I just know I want to be saved in You, my Lord.

I want to hold onto You like never before, no matter where my life takes me.

O Lord, I want to truly stay grounded in Your holy word day after day.

I want life to take me on a closer walk with You, my Lord Jesus Christ, who is beyond just talk in life.

A Day Can Make Us Feel

A sunny day can perk us up and make us feel good all day long.

A rainy day can make us feel down and not care about being late to wherever we need to go.

A warm day can make us feel great in many ways.

The holy Sabbath day of rest can make us feel close to the Lord and feel so refreshed if we keep the Sabbath day holy before our Lord Jesus Christ.

He has the power to make a day what he wants it to be for our good.

We might not always see what He does, but we should always give Jesus the glory and praise.

What We Believe

What we believe we will say in words, whether they're good or bad, day after day.

What we believe we will do and it will show in our actions that people will see more than a little bit.

What we believe will mold and shape our lives to be good or bad, no matter how old or young we are.

What we believe will show and tell in our lives so we will not be deceived and will reap what we sow.

What we believe to be the truth or a lie, Jesus will truly always know.

We can believe in Jesus Christ, who will save us from our sins.

What Can We Call Our Own?

What can we call our own when a hurricane blows it all down upon the land?

What can we call our own when a fire burns it all up to the last wire?

What can we call our own when a flood of water can damage it all and leave behind a ton of mud?

What can we call our own when an earthquake crumbles it all down at any hour of the day?

The only thing we can call our own is our free will choice. With that, we can choose Jesus Christ as our Lord and savior or the devil as our ruin.

Life will only show us favor when we believe in Jesus Christ, our Lord and savior.

Jesus will call us his own if we are saved in Him.

You Keep a Record

O, Lord, you keep a record of our thoughts that the devil doesn't know, no matter where we are.

You, O Lord, keep a record of every word we say, whether they're words of love or words of hate.

You, O Lord, always hear everything day after day, week after week and year after year.

You, Lord Jesus, keep a record of our actions whether they are actions of grudges or actions of compassion.

There is nothing that You don't see.

You, O Lord, know how to set us free with the truth of your holy word.

It is filled with You, who keeps a record of everything that we do all of our life long days, which are only a few to You.

Only One True Living God

There is only one true living God. Idol gods can't love you because they have no hearts to love with.

There is only one true living God. Idol gods can't bless you and me to do good in life, that has only one true living God.

Idol gods can't heal you from sickness and disease.

The only one under the sun and beyond the sun who can do this is the one true living God.

Idol gods have no heaven to put you in because there is only one true living God who can do that.

Idol gods can't forgive you and cleanse you of your sins.

Jesus Christ is one with God to be the true living god.

Idol gods can't give you and me life, health and strength with the truth to set us free.

Only the true living God can do that, but the spiritually blind can't see this truth.

I am a Pilgrim

I am a pilgrim passing through a foreign, sinful world.

I am born again in the spiritual birth of my Lord and savior Jesus Christ, who is before the heavens and earth.

I am a pilgrim passing through a world of sin that will pass away one day.

I will be with Jesus beyond this strange world that I see being only temporary for me to pass through with my brothers and sisters in Jesus Christ.

Jesus says to love one another in this foreign, sinful world where a pilgrim of Jesus Christ will pass through this savage last days to receive eternal life.

A Sincere Prayer

God loves a sincere prayer from the heart that's true.

God is not impressed with an intelligent prayer.

You and I can't outsmart God in our prayers; they must be sincere to God whether we pray out loud or from within our thoughts.

God will always see whether we're sincere or not, whether we pray many words or just a few.

A few words can be enough for God to hear and answer so sincere for you and me.

We can't fool God with a charming prayer that can sound so good to listening ears, especially on God's holy ground.

God loves a sincere prayer that a little child can pray to God and touch His heart day after day.

Which Direction Will We Go?

Which direction will we go when the Lord wakes us up in the morning to see another day beyond the dust of the earth?

We can go here and there on roads that seem to have no end in direction.

There is only one direction that leads to heaven above the dead-end road to hell for all who are lost because of not walking in the spirit of God who is leading us in the direction of Jesus Christ.

He is the way, the truth and the life with no end and will always direct you and me to be saved in His grace.

His grace will lead you and me to keep God's commandments if we love Jesus so real.

He wants us to go in the direction of living a renewed life.

Jesus Christ walked in the direction of death on the cross to pay or price.

We have a choice to take the direction leading us to our destiny.

We will choose our destiny all along by what we say and do.

Some Things We Must Leave Alone

Some things we must leave alone and let them be buried under some stones.

Some things in the past we must leave alone, especially if they didn't have a bad effect on someone's life and cause misery.

Judas betrayed Jesus, who was arrested.

His disciples ran away and scattered, and did not pass Jesus' test.

Jesus didn't hold that against them. He left it alone and didn't address it to anyone.

Some things we must leave alone, and not dig up something that's been buried a long time ago.

Around the clock someone will say something about what happened in the past years that should be left alone.

Children don't usually have a fear of doing immature foolish things and even a lot of teenagers can do immature things to regret it years to come. Some things we will not understand should be left alone, as long as they don't ruin someone's life

Leaving some things alone is a good thing to do.

Jesus Christ, our Lord, gave up His life to save us from our sins and not to condemn us in our sins all through our lives.

My Life Is Not About Me

My life is not about me. Jesus put me here to be about Him by loving and obeying Him who sets me free from me.

My life is not about me. Jesus put me here to love my neighbors like I love myself, and I am not able to do anything good without Jesus, from which all good things come.

My life is not about me. Jesus put me here under the sun to do His holy will, not my own will that makes me selfish and not care about how others may feel.

My life is not about me. Jesus Christ, my Lord, put me here to be a blessing to others day after day and year after year.

My life is not about me. Jesus put me here to deny myself and pick up my cross and follow Him who cannot lie to me.

My life is not about me. Jesus put me here to swallow my pride and not to believe that I am better than someone else whose eyes may be stayed on Jesus.

My eyes can look away from Jesus if I am looking at people's faults and sins every day.

My life is not about me. Jesus put me here to keep my eyes on Him because with out Him I am like a lost sheep in the wilderness

If We Hold Onto Jesus

If we hold onto Jesus, we will grow in faith and believe in Jesus more and more to take on the world.

If we hold on to Jesus, we will grow in wisdom and make more and more good choices wherever we go.

If we hold on to Jesus, we will grow in knowledge of the truth of God's holy word.

If we hold onto Jesus, we will grow in love to give more and more of our heart to Jesus Christ, who we can always hold onto and will never regret it in our life.

If we hold on to Jesus, we will grow in grace, giving us more and more of Jesus to save us from our sins.

Number One

There are people who want to be number one in what they do, and they will give you a bad name if you get in their way.

Being number one is what many people live for under the sun, where pride can truly swell anyone's head in the church.

Some church folks want to be number one for their ministry work, and be the best and better than the rest.

Being number one can impress people, but it can't impress the Lord Jesus Christ, who loves a humble heart.

Being humble is the best thing to Jesus every day.

If the Lord gives you a talent to be number one in what you do, make it all about Him who always sees who can handle being number one and not let it go to their heads.

Jesus is number one in all that He does to save us from our sins

Do Good Things in Jesus' Name

Some people will try to discourage you and me from doing good things in Jesus' name.

We can agree on that in every way.

It's always good to do good things for Jesus' name's sake.

There is no mistake, and every born again believer in Jesus Christ knows this.

The devil hates to see us doing good things in our lives.

Doing good things in man's name can leave a question mark, for the answer is not always right upon the land.

Man's name will fall short of the glory of God and that's how it is with our name that cannot always stand up against the devil like Jesus' name can.

You and I can always do good things in Jesus' holy name, which has no sin upon it while our names have more than a little bit of sin on them.

Our Name is Precious to Jesus

Our name is precious to Jesus, who knows our name like a love song to Him. He loves our names all the same, and they are precious to Him all day long and all night long.

Jesus calls us by our names that belong to Him who is strong and mighty. Our names are precious to Jesus Christ who loves you and me.

We don't have to think twice about it when someone calls our name.

Our name is like music to the Lord who loves us all and wants to write our names in His book of life.

The holy and precious name of Jesus Christ is heaven to all who are saved in His holy name that has no blemish and no blame.

Our names are so precious to Jesus each and every day, as he calls us by them, asking us to follow Him all the way.

There is Nothing You Can't Do

There is nothing you can't do for me, O Lord.

I can put all of my trust in You who sees and foresees my future days that are in Your almighty hands.

If it's in Your will, O Lord, I will see those future days in the land of the living.

There is nothing that you can't do for me, Lord Jesus.

You have brought me through all of my past days that I don't deserve, and I am so glad to see this day and to be alive.

The devil is so mad when he sees me doing so well, especially in doing Your will, O Lord.

You can't fail me, from my birth to my old age that is a blessing from you, my Lord and Savior Jesus Christ.

There is nothing that You can't do for me in my life, O Lord who will supply all of my needs.

I don't have to worry about anything, because nothing is too hard for You to see and no problem too difficult for You to solve.

There is nothing that You can't do for me, O Lord, even if I am on my dying bed.

I know that I will one day live again when you come back.

Help Me to Represent You

Help me represent You, my Lord and Savior Jesus Christ.

I want to represent You, O Lord, so people will see you in my life wherever I go here and there.

Help me to represent You, so people will see You in my eyes because they get no judgmental looks from me.

Help me to represent You, O Lord, in what I say to people so they hear kind words from the tip of my tongue every day.

Help me to represent You, my Lord, in what I do, so that my actions will be about You and represent You all through my life.

When people look at me, I want them to see You, O Lord, who can set anyone free from being selfish.

O Lord, You brought me a long way so I could see this day and love You and my neighbors.

I want to represent You, my Lord Jesus, who's always able to change my heart so I can confess and repent of my sins.

Help me to represent You, O Lord, even when I just don't know what effect I will have on someone in my presence.

You, O Lord, Gave Me

I was wandering in life, for I had no hope, no focus and no dreams. I was like a sinking boat.

I wandered through my life, not knowing who I was or where I was going.

The Lord showed His mercy on me, called me into His flock and gave me all that I needed to be His child.

You, O Lord, gave me hope and let me smile, even when I am feeling down.

You, O Lord, gave me focus on Your holy ground, so I know that Your love is all around me.

You, O Lord, gave me a dream beyond my wandering life that had no beams of light.

You, O Lord, gave me a water stream of your forgiveness and goodness leading me to repent.

The Most Beautiful House

The most beautiful house has a glorious rooftop that can reach up to heaven where holy angels love to worship and obey Jesus Christ forever, non-stop.

The foundation is more stable than the planets and stars that are so far away from this world and galaxies afar.

The windows will sparkle brighter than any gemstone, and the doors are higher than the mountains with a lock and master key that belongs to Jesus alone.

Every piece of furniture is more beautiful than rainbows that arch high up in the sky and down in the corners of the world's ocean floors below.

King Solomon could never build a better house so fine.

The most beautiful house is the heart that loves Jesus all of the time.

Jesus will always keep the blueprints in His heart.

Jesus is the Living, Open Door

Anybody can walk through the living door with a true repentant heart, confessing every sin.

Jesus will accept you and me just the way we are.

Jesus will add us to His number that no man can count, like all the stars.

Jesus is the only living door that we can walk through to be saved in His amazing grace before we go to the grave.

We can walk through the living door that is always open wide to accept us in God's holy house each and every day.

There is another door that anyone can walk through of no return to head straight into the lake of fire that will greatly burn.

One day soon, the living door will close on all who don't want to come into the house of prayer, no matter being great or small.

We don't have to knock on the living door that is still open until God says to close it, and that will surely happen so real.

Jesus says, "I am the living door that you can walk through today before the last hour runs out on you."

The Bridge of Eternity

Many are called, but only a few are chosen to walk hand in hand with Jesus across the bridge of eternity into the heavenly holy land.

The few chosen will cross over the sea of sin that Jesus will one day bring to an everlasting end.

Immortality will stretch out her loving arms from heaven above, and wrap them around all the saints with God's unchangeable love.

There is an eternal land of sweet by and by for all who love and obey Jesus with no heart of deny.

The bridge of eternity is forever far away, and only Jesus Christ can lead us across it one day.

Beyond Science

Beyond science are the prophecies in the bible that will be fulfilled by God, who used holy men to write His book of all truth.

Science has a lot of truth, but not like bible truth that is always reliable to believe all through our lives.

The bible has already predicted what science has to say about a lot of things.

Science predicts that global warming will cause more and more hurricanes, floods, heat waves, droughts, wild fires and tornadoes.

This makes the bible true when it talks about in these last days; there will be perilous times.

Beyond science there is no mistake in God's holy word.

Science can make some mistakes that we can see, and will not always be in line with God's word that will never change.

Science can go through some changes when something new is discovered. Science can't rise above the Lord.

The Lord Jesus Christ will always be beyond science.

He was before science and he will be after science that will one day pass away with this sinful world.

It Blows My Mind

It blows my mind that Jesus took on all of my temptations.

It blows my mind that Jesus took on all of my flaws that are bad.

It blows my mind that Jesus took on all of my bad habits.

It blows my mind that Jesus Christ took on all of my bad hereditary tendencies through the price He paid on the cross for all of my sins.

It blows my mind that Jesus took on all of my bad motives and intentions that are sad things to Jesus.

It blows my mind that Jesus took on all of my bad ways.

It blows my mind that Jesus took on all of my bad thoughts that look like a dried up brook to Him.

It blows my mind that Jesus took on all of my small-minded bad words.

It blows my mind that Jesus took on all of my bad actions that are like a crook to Him.

It blows my mind that Jesus took on all of my sins that I deserve to die in. His love blows my mind every day.

Nothing can rise above Jesus.

In Church

There are some people in church because they want to make a name for themselves.

Some people are in church for what they do in the church.

There are some people in church who don't love all the truth and will dislike me and you if we step on their toes with the truth.

Some people in the church will show clicks and some people in the church have some tricks up their sleeves.

There are some people in the church who are proud and there are some people in the church who are loud.

Some people in church are set in their old ways.

Some people in the church believe they are perfect in every way and believe they have no sins to confess and repent of.

Any church that doesn't love Jesus Christ is full of pretense that Jesus will shove away from Him.

There are some people in church who truly love and obey Jesus and are humble in their ministry work and do not boast about themselves.

A church that is about pleasing Jesus Christ will be blessed with an abundance of life.

It's the Holy Spirit

It's the Holy Spirit that is the still quiet voice who speaks the truth to our conscious and gets it back on the right course.

It's the Holy Spirit who makes us feel guilty for saying wrong words and doing wrong things that's aren't like Jesus, who is forever strong and mighty in righteousness.

It's the Holy Spirit who will always tell us the truth about everyone and everything.

It's the Holy Spirit who changes our lives to live for Jesus Christ, who will always do us good and well.

It's the Holy Spirit who reveals to us the mysteries of God all through the bible.

It's the Holy Spirit who gives us the understanding of God's holy word and God's love.

Jesus was born of a virgin mother and born of the Holy Spirit to live a sinless life upon the land.

It was the Holy Spirit who was with God the Father and Son at the creation of Adam and Eve.

Forever beyond this world, it was the Holy Spirit in on the creation of angels in Heaven where the Holy Spirit is a part of the Trinity Godhead.

The Holy Spirit was in on the creation of all things except sin.

The Best Way

The best way to overcome fears is to face up to them with the help of the Lord, who is so dear to us.

The best way to encourage others is to encourage yourself with the help of the Lord, who loves to encourage you and me.

The best way to love is to love Jesus Christ, and love your neighbor as you love yourself in this life.

The best way to live is to live by God's holy word every day.

There is no better way to live, just like the bible says.

The best way to die is to die being saved in Jesus Christ, who got the victory over death and the grave.

The best way to resist the devil's temptations is to pray to Jesus and ask Him for strength right away.

The best way to be a witness of Jesus and win souls is to keep His Ten Commandments wherever we go.

If I Was Rich

If I was rich, there would be a lot more phony people in my life.

All I need is to be spiritually rich in the Lord.

If I was rich, a lot more people would tell me lies.

All I need to be is spiritually rich in people's eyes.

If I was rich, a lot more people would be jealous of me.

All I need is to be spiritually rich in the Lord who sees all of my friends and enemies.

If I was rich, a lot more people would try to use me every day.

All I need is to be spiritually rich in the Lord who I can pray to and ask Him to use me in a way that is always good for my soul.

If I was rich, a lot more people would want to be my friend.

All I need is to be spiritually rich in Jesus Christ, who can save me from my sins, when friends can turn their backs on me until my life comes to an end.

Real Life Can Be Complicated

A romantic movie can really be good, with all the scenes looking so right, but it's not real life.

Real life can be complicated for many people, who leave love to pursue their dreams over love that nothing can rise above.

Real life can be complicated each and every day.

Many people make it complicated to love Jesus, who is the way, the truth and the life that is never complicated to live.

Many people are doing their own will, which makes their life complicated so real.

It's so easy to watch a love story that's make-believe, where a couple in love will get a happy ending.

In real life, we can see that many people will leave their spouse to follow their dreams.

Real life can be complicated under the sunlight beams, where love can be taken for granted.

Many people will take Jesus' love for granted on this planet, where real life can be complicated and can cause you and me panic with so much doubt.

Jesus is always so plain and clear with His love that can move hearts to repent so simple and dear.

The Kind of World We Live In

There are people that will give you and me the evil eye look if we don't look like them.

There are people who are making millions of dollars for joking about people, even though it may be true.

This is the kind of world we live in.

What we need is for everyone to confess and repent of their sins unto Jesus Christ.

There are people whose hearts may be changing to serve the Lord.

This is the kind of world that we live in under the stars where every man, woman, boy and girl belongs to Jesus, who also owns this world we live in.

There are many people who are friends to this world and not a friend to Jesus, who is a friend to all who will love and obey Him.

He can change people's lives and give them a much better than slim chance to make it to heaven above.

This is the kind of world we live in.

We may get shoved around in sin, but it can't shove around God's love for us.

We Are

We are what we say, whether we say good words or bad words day after day.

We are what we do, whether we do pure things or corrupt things.

We never see all the good things that Jesus can do.

We are our motives to be selfless or selfish.

We are about Jesus Christ or we are about the devil in our lives.

There is no in-between about who we are to Jesus, who knows all of our hearts.

We are living the truth of Jesus or we are living a lie of the devil. Either way, God always sees.

Who's to Say?

Who's to say that you won't succeed in anything in life?

The Lord can truly see that you can succeed.

Who's to say that you won't get anywhere in life?

The Lord can always lead you here and there to get somewhere in life. Who's to say that you won't amount to anything in life?

The Lord can surely get you through when you've fallen short in life.

Who's to say that you won't bounce back in life?

The Lord can truly make your life much better — so exact and on time.

Who's to say that you will fail in life?

The Lord can surely give you the victory so very nice.

Who's to say you only have a short time to live?

The Lord can truly prolong your life if it's in His will.

Who's to say that you won't be saved?

The Lord can truly save you before you go to the grave.

Who's to say that you are not free?

The Lord gave you a free will choice so you can choose to follow Him and not be lost.

Only About This Life

Many people will live only about this life, when the eternal life is to live for Jesus Christ.

Many people will live only about this life here on earth, when there is a perfect after life without a doubt in Jesus Christ, who's above this life here on earth.

Day after day and year after year, many people will live only about this life that is short lived, compared to eternal life in Jesus, who is forevermore real than anything in this life on earth.

Many people will work themselves to death for this life that can make us short of breath, but Jesus is the breath of life to prolong our days into many years if it's in His will.

Being only about this life is the way that many people will go, but that only leads to a dead end, but Jesus can save us from our sins and promise us eternal life.

Many people will die being only about this life, causing them to be lost.

The Lord is about giving us eternal life when we make Him our choice over this life that has no course to eternity.

Just Because

Just because someone is younger than you, it doesn't mean that he or she will live longer than you.

Just because someone is older than you, it doesn't mean that he or she is more mature than you.

Just because someone is smarter than you, it doesn't mean that he or she will use their common sense like you.

Just because someone has more money than you, it doesn't make him or her better than you.

Just because someone is bigger than you, it doesn't make him or her stronger than you.

Just because someone is smaller than you, it doesn't mean he or she is less healthy than you.

Just because someone is more friendly than you, it doesn't make him or her more giving than you.

Just because someone goes to church on time more than you, it doesn't mean that he or she will get more of the Lord's favor than you.

Just because someone talks more than you, it doesn't mean that he or she has more experience in life than you.

Just because someone is more loving than you, it doesn't mean that he or she will get more of the Lord's love than you.

We Must Keep Ourselves Busy for the Lord

We must keep ourselves busy for the Lord, as if Jesus will come back today to tell us, "You have done well in my will that is eternal."

We must keep ourselves busy in using our gifts that the Lord gave us to build up His church and uplift the saints.

To hold onto Jesus Christ, we must keep ourselves busy in loving Him and loving one another so we won't spiritually sleepwalk into the walls of sin.

We must keep ourselves busy in winning souls to Jesus, who gives us talents to not be buried in selfishness wherever we go.

We must keep ourselves busy for the Lord by being good to everyone and treating everyone right under the beautiful bright sun.

So many people are busy for the devil every day.

There are criminals who may never be caught because many people do not really care.

We must keep ourselves busy keeping God's golden rules. We will not get tired of keeping them if we love Jesus, who kept His Heavenly Father's holy law when he lived on earth without sin.

We must keep ourselves busy for the Lord first, before being busy doing anything else that can empty the wallet and purse with no blessings from the Lord.

Jesus was about His Heavenly Father's business when He lived on earth without sin.

The After Life

The after life is the eternal life that Jesus will give to us when He comes back again.

There is no other after life that only Jesus Christ can give us if we are saved in Him before we die.

We can't put our trust in this life that is short to make us old before we know it.

The after life is the real true life to live forever and ever with the Lord, whose holy word is like a double-edged sword.

This life here on earth is like a fairy tale that is told, and like a shadow that passes over the landscape.

We can be here today and gone tomorrow so far away from the land of the living.

The after life in Jesus Christ is what we can hope for through the price that Jesus paid for our sins on the cross.

This life can pretend to be nice to us with its short lifespan that will bring us to an end as if we never lived.

A few people will live a few years over one hundred years old, but that is short lived to the Lord.

The afterlife is what Jesus promised to all who love and obey Him in this life that's short lived.

We Don't Know What We Are Made Of

We don't know what we are made of until someone says something to us that we don't like to hear on any day.

We don't know what we are made of until someone does something to us that we don't like and we show our true self, whether getting revenge or letting it go.

We don't know what we are made of until we lose a loved one who's so dear to us.

Jesus knows what we are made of, even before we were born to choose to love or hate.

We don't know what we are made of until we lose everything that we have, then others will see if we are strong or weak.

Jesus Christ the Lord knows what we are made of in this sinful world below the heavens.

We don't know what we are made of until someone gets on our last nerve. Jesus knows what we are made of and can give us the power to not give into our flesh that is weak.

We don't know what we are made of until we are facing up to death.

We love to live our life that we don't want to fade away into the dust of the earth.

Jesus always knows what we are made of.

We don't fully know our own hearts, but Jesus knows that from the start to the end of our lives.

We Say We Are Christians

We say we are Christians.

Do we shine like the full white moonlight looking so mysterious in the night?

Do we look so mysterious in our Christianity that someone can't solve us and figure out we're Christians?

We say we are Christians.

Do we shine like the stores' parking lot lights in the night?

They don't shine so bright for someone to always see, like a criminal lurking there to rob us.

People need to see the light of Jesus in you.

We say we are Christians.

Do we shine like the streetlights in the night?

They don't have a lot of light for us to not meet another driver head on to cause a crash.

Is our Christianity crashing into anyone who needs to see the light of Jesus Christ living in us?

We say we are Christians.

We should be shining bright like the sunlight.

The people of the world should see that we are different from them wherever we go, day or night.

We say we are Christians.

Do we turn our Christianity on and off to people?

We say we are Christians upon this sinful land where our Christianity doesn't have anyone's freewill choice on our hands.

Time Needs a Promotion

Time needs a promotion because time works hard for many people to get a good education.

Time gives us more time to get all of our hearts right with the Lord.

Time should always be recognized for its good works

It deserves the best promotion on earth.

Time is a gift to us from God who gives us borrowed time to live and do His holy will.

No business will ever think about promoting time that is this world's best employee under the sunshine.

Time works harder than everyone else every day

Time needs a pay raise that no business can afford in any way.

Time will get its promotion from the Lord for giving us all the time to repent of our sins while we are living.

Time will be too late for many people who refuse to do what the Lord commands.

Time works hard for you and me to be saved in Jesus Christ.

Time has a union to represent time for being good to us in this life.

Many young people are killed. Many babies are dying.

Can we question their very short time on earth and get the answer that may leave us speechless?

If the Lord Is Not In

The leaves will fall off the trees in the fall season.

Our reasons can fall into nonsense if the Lord is not in our reasoning.

The strong hurricanes and tornado winds can blow some trees down.

Strong negative words can blow someone's good name down.

If the Lord is not in what we do, we will be like the ground soaked with water to breed a lot of mosquitoes.

We will be like the leaves that can fade on a tree if the Lord is not in our lives for us to do His will.

Like a wild hungry animal searching for food, you and I are searching for temporary things.

If the Lord is not in our search, we won't find anything worth holding on top in this world.

If the Lord Jesus Christ is not in our coming and going here and there. we are like a bird flying into a trap.

We are like the deep woods, having no path if the Lord is not in our daily walk and talk.

We can choose to put the Lord in our lives so that we can have peace of mind in this ugly, troubled world.

Compared to the Eternal Life

This life is short compared to the eternal life we can only receive through our Lord Jesus Christ.

This life is nothing to treasure compared to the eternal life that all who are saved in Jesus will live.

This life is injustice and nothing to reason with compared to the eternal life that has no treasons of unpredictability and uncertainty.

This life is like a bad dream compared to the eternal life that has an eternal reality of good things going on so very nice for all who make it to heaven one day.

This life is useless and wasteful compared to the eternal life that is filled with great things for you and me to do in Jesus' holy and precious name.

This life has many broken promises and many more to break compared to the eternal life that Jesus Christ the Lord has promised to all who are saved in Him before He comes back again.

Sickness and Death

Sickness and death don't care about how young or old that you are to take you out of life.

Sickness and death don't care about how rich or poor that you are.

They will take you down into a deep ditch that's filled with the dirty water and mud of sorrow.

Sickness and death don't care about you being good or evil. They will never be on your side in no matter what neighborhood you live in.

Sickness and death don't care about how wise or how foolish you are. They show no favoritism.

Sickness and death don't care about you being educated or not educated. They will make you feel miserable around the clock.

Jesus Christ is the life eternal over sickness and death, for Jesus is all that you and I have left after this life is over.

He is the only way that will one day live again.

Jesus is coming back one day soon to put an end to sickness and death.

All of the righteous will have their victory over sickness and death when we see Jesus on the clouds of glory.

It Takes a Lot to Live

It takes a lot to live, but it doesn't take a lot to make a mistake.

It takes a lot to live, but it doesn't take a lot to say something wrong on any day.

It takes a lot to live, but it doesn't take a lot to do something wrong at any hour on the clock.

It takes a lot to live, but it doesn't take a lot to die, with the graveyard waiting before our eyes.

It takes a lot to live unto the Lord Jesus Christ, but it doesn't take a lot to sin against Him who paid our price on the cross to save us from our sins.

It takes a lot to live, but it doesn't take a lot to shorten our lives if we live in rebellion against God, who is love and not strife.

It takes a lot to live, but it doesn't take a lot to be selfish and do our own thing no matter who is watching.

It takes a lot to live, but it doesn't take a lot to cause our health to go bad in the winter, spring, summer or fall season.

To be a God

It's easy to make money to be a God.

It's easy to make a human being to be a God.

It's easy to make a job to be a God.

It's easy to make technology to be a God.

It's easy to make science to be a God.

It's easy to make an animal to be a God.

It's easy to make a talent to be a God.

It's easy to make nature to be a God.

It's easy to make oneself to be a God.

It's easy to make a car to be a God.

It's easy to make a house to be a God.

It's easy to make clothes to be a God.

It's easy to make material things to be a God.

It's easy to make temporary things to be a God.

It's easy to make the true living God not our God.

It's easy to make this world to be a God.

Do We Ever?

Do we ever throw a tantrum at God if we can't get our way with Him who knows all of our hearts?

Do we ever try to outsmart God, whose intelligence is infinite beyond all the stars?

Do we ever try to run away from God, who will always catch us in His holy word that he speaks to us every day?

Do we ever wrestle with God, whose strength can crush mountains down on you and me?

Do we ever try to beat up God if He doesn't answer our prayers?

Do you and I ever break bad at God by not doing something He wants us to do?

God can humble us so everyone can see that He is God.

Do we ever try to challenge God to get our own way that God doesn't trust?

Do we ever try to compare ourselves with God's son, Jesus Christ, who was born without sin?

We are not free of sin in this life.

We need Jesus to forgive us of our sins and save us so we can one day live with God.

As Long as I Do Your Will

As long as I do your will, O Lord, You will show me things that I can do in Your holy name so that I can see that You are there for me.

As long as I do your will, O Lord, You will bless me and see to all of my needs, filling my life with contentment.

As long as I do your will, my Lord, You will give me the strength to stay on board and follow Your will, which is always good for my soul.

As long as I do your will, O Lord, You will go with me no matter what I go through in my life.

As long as I do your will, my Lord and Savior Jesus Christ, You will save me from being lost in my sins.

As long as I do your will, O Lord, You will be my best friend who I can always love and trust until my life ends.

As long as I do your will, My Lord Jesus, You will shelter me through the storms that can do me injustice in a world where there is nothing new under the sun.

So Amazing

The Lord is so amazing all the time.

He can do anything but fail under the sunshine.

The Lord is so amazing that he can make something good out of something bad on any day.

The Lord is so amazing to bless our lives to prosper so very nice with the price He paid on the cross for our sins.

The Lord is so amazing from the beginning to the end of the day, week, month, and year.

He will answer our prayers if we love and obey Him so dear.

Our Lord and Savior Jesus Christ is so amazing to cleanse us of our sins if we confess and repent unto Him with a sincere heart.

The Lord is so amazing to make a hard problem small enough to swallow down so we can continue living and loving Him.

You and I Can Choose

The wind cannot choose the direction it will blow in.

The rain cannot choose where it will fall.

But, you and I can choose to trust Jesus to be our best friend.

A tree cannot choose to grow tall.

The leaves on a tree cannot choose to change their color.

But, you and I can choose to love one another.

The seasons cannot choose to change.

An animal cannot choose to think in its brain.

But, you and I can choose to think about Jesus Christ.

A snake cannot choose to be nice.

Whatever we buy cannot choose to give us a price.

But, you and I can choose to do God's will rather than our own.

A mystery cannot choose to give us a clue.

Money cannot choose to make anyone rich.

But, you and I can choose to shorten our lives and lick the dust.

And, you and I can choose to repent of our sins and live our lives unto Jesus before our lives end.

The Lord Can Give Us the Strength

The Lord can give us the strength to overcome depression.

The Lord can give us the strength to overcome stress.

The Lord can give us the strength to overcome disappointment.

The Lord can give us the strength to overcome worries.

The Lord can give us the strength to overcome fears.

The Lord can give us the strength to overcome heartaches.

The Lord can give us the strength to overcome loneliness.

The Lord can give us the strength to overcome grief.

The Lord can give us the strength to overcome pride.

The Lord can give us the strength to overcome selfishness.

If we ask the Lord for strength, He will give us strength if we believe in Him.

We have no strength within ourselves to overcome anything in this world. The Lord is our strength that we can depend on to help us to overcome any problem.

The Sound of Life

The sound of life is in the wind that blows through the trees.

The sound of life is the rain that falls on the rooftops covering over you and me.

The sound of life is the horn blowing on the train.

The sound of life is someone calling our name.

The sound of life is the ocean waves splashing on the water's surface.

The sound of life is a storm that rages.

The sound of life is a factory making noise.

The sound of life is hearing someone's voice.

The sound of life is a baby talking and a baby crying.

The sound of life is millstone grinding and coal mining.

The sound of life is talking, laughing, and singing.

The sound of life is the bells ringing.

The sound of life is preaching sermons about Jesus Christ.

The sound of life is teaching and singing songs about Jesus, who is life eternal.

The sound of life is giving a testimony about Jesus Christ.

The sound of life is shouting for joy that Jesus paid our price.

A Spiritual Good Flavor

We are the salt of the earth to give the world a spiritual good flavor of Jesus who so loved us first.

We are the salt of the earth to season this world with the gospel of Jesus Christ who is our reason for being a Christian.

We are the salt of the earth to give this world a good taste of the love of God who gave us His Son, Jesus, to save our souls.

A good spiritual flavor is what this world truly needs every day.

Jesus is the life, the truth and the way to live our lives.

Jesus has seasoned the church with a good spiritual flavor to let the world know that He is our Lord and Savior.

People love to have a good flavor on their food for it to taste so good as they chew it up and swallow it down.

Jesus came to this world to give a good service to this world with His right example for us to live by.

He shows every man, woman, boy and girl what they can do by loving Him.

He will save His children of salt all over this world.

To a Desolate Place

Jesus will take us to a desolate place in our walk with Him, who sees us to be faithful beyond our talk.

Jesus will take us to a desolate place in our relationship with Him, who sees if we love Him beyond the tip of our tongues.

Jesus will take us to a desolate place in our minds to think on Him, who is always on time.

Jesus will take us to a desolate place in our hearts to feel His Holy Spirit mending our pain that is hard for us to do.

Jesus will take us to a desolate place in our lives for us to keep our eyes on Him day after day.

Jesus will take us to a desolate place in our trials for us to trust Him to bring us through what may only take a little while.

Jesus takes us to these desolate places as a blessing to teach us a good lesson.

Jesus takes us through our testing times to make Him shine.

Won't Control Us

The sun won't control us to see its light.

The moon won't control us to see its glow in the night.

The sky won't control us to see that it's always opened wide.

Jesus won't control us to be by His side.

The air won't control us to breathe it in and out.

Jesus won't control us to be about Him, who we should never doubt.

There are people who will try to control you and me.

Jesus won't control us; he wants to set us free.

The ground won't control us to walk or run on it.

Jesus won't control us the least bit.

Nature won't control us with its presence of peace.

Jesus won't control us from the north, south, west, or east.

There are people who will try to control us like crabs pulling one another down in a barrel.

Jesus won't control any man, woman, boy or girl.

The rain won't control us to get wet.

Jesus won't control us to love and obey Him no matter where we are at.

There are people who will try to control us with claws like a cat,

Jesus won't control us to do or say this or that.

Jesus gives us all a free will that the devil wants us to forget.

The devil loves to control anyone to do evil.

We have a free will to let Jesus in our hearts.

We Exist

We exist from the birth of our mother's womb.

So many people don't exist anymore beneath the grave tomb.

God created Adam and Eve for us all to exist today.

God created two human beings to populate this world like the bible says.

The living exist because of Jesus Christ, who laid down His life and rose from the grave for us to live a renewed life in doing His holy will that the dead can't do.

Beyond Adam and Eve, we exist today because of Jesus.

He is the reason we live to see this day that the dead don't see.

To exist is a blessing from the Lord God who can be everywhere all around the world, throughout the universe, and all across the heavens where God existed first.

We exist to love and obey Jesus Christ, the Son of God, whose existence is eternal beyond all the stars.

Nothing can exist without God.

A man can believe he can exist without God, but he is truly deceived.

A Love Letter to Life

I can live my life like I will live forever.

You let me know so very clever that tomorrow is not promised to me.

I love You, Lord, for helping me to see the truth of my life.

You will take me through some changes that I must accept from You for as long as I live.

You are from the Lord Jesus Christ, who is the way, the truth and the life.

You love to live in everyone.

Everyone will not love you and will degrade you twenty-four hours around the clock.

You, my life, love the Lord.

Death hates you more and more.

A love letter to life is a great reward for all the living to love and obey the Lord.

You make Your plans for me to live a long life.

My bad choices can insult Your plans and cut You like a sharp knife.

Your presence is so good to see in the land of the living.

No one can beat God's giving ways that life truly knows every day.

You Are Not Finished with Me Yet

I am so glad that you are not finished with me yet.

You, O Lord, show me that you have more for me to do.

You, O Lord, are not finished using me who loves to always be used by You.

You will never cause me to feel bad for being used by You.

You, my Lord and Savior Jesus Christ, are not finished blessing me to live my life all about doing Your holy will.

I am so glad that you are not finished with me yet.

Your love for me is so real, no matter where I am in my life.

Whenever I think that You are finished with me, You show me that you are not.

Keep on using me before my biological clock runs out, O Lord.

I know You are not finished with me yet, and nobody can change that.

Real, True Living

Real, true living is living right unto the Lord, who can make our lives so well protected before we say one word.

Real, true living is to avoid doing evil deeds against our neighbors, who we should love more and more.

Real, true living is to labor for the Lord, who we can't beat giving.

Real, true living is to love and obey our Lord and Savior Jesus Christ, day after day.

Real, true living is not to worry about dying when the Lord has the victory over death that is not the end of our destiny.

Our destiny will be heaven if we are saved in Jesus Christ, who is the bright and morning star.

Real, true living is living our lives with a peace of mind no matter what we go through.

Jesus is always on time to bless our lives if we live our life unto Him who is always so divine.

There is an Eternal Place

There is an eternal place where all the saints will one day go.

That eternal place is beyond the outer space that will blow our minds when we go there one day.

There is an eternal place where our dreams cannot trace and cannot embrace the face of God.

There is an eternal place that Jesus Christ, our Lord, is preparing for you and me after our lives have been renewed through the righteousness of Jesus who can never do wrong.

That eternal place is heaven above this sinful world where there are many places that are so corrupt with evil that we can't bear to live in.

There is an eternal place that all the saints can relate to, no matter whether they're great or small, because God loves all of His holy saints the same.

There is an eternal place that will forever exist in Jesus' name, which has no blemishes and no blame.

It is an eternal place above the sun, moon and stars, where there is an eternal God who loves a faithful heart.

But What About in Between

We come into this world naked and we will leave this world naked, but what about in between?

The Lord will supply all of our needs.

We come into this world naked and we will leave this world naked, but what about in between?

We can believe in Jesus Christ to be saved from our sins so we can be set free.

We come into this world naked and we will leave this world naked, but what about in between?

Every man, woman, boy and girl can love and obey the Lord Jesus Christ.

We come into this world naked and we will leave this world naked but what about in between?

We can cast our pearls before our brothers and sisters in the household of faith.

We come into this world naked and we will leave this world naked, but what about in between?

We can do good and not evil to touch God's heart.

We come into this world naked and we will leave this world naked, but what about in between?

We can love one another to cut up the devil's hate in this world.

Way Beyond Dreams in the Night

Heaven is way beyond dreams in the night.

We are unconscious in our deep sleep being so right for our mind and body to rest in good dreams beneath the heavens on high.

Jesus lives beyond the songs we sing about Him in the early morning, evening and in the midnight hour of our trials.

Jesus holds them in his hand, way beyond dreams in the night under the heavens on high above all the streetlights shining so well known in our eyes.

We will one day see Jesus Christ on the clouds of glory.

He will take us to heaven with Him for a thousand years, but only if you and I are saved in Him.

Jesus is happy to save us, way beyond dreams in the night that will rush to get a reservation in heaven to be with Jesus Christ, who's forevermore real beyond dreams, that can be so nice and mean to us in our sleep in the night under the full white moonlight.

God's Eyes

God's eyes are like the sunlight in the day, and God's eyes are like the full moonlight in the night, way above our eyes.

We can't see all over this world like God's all-seeing eyes that will never overlook anyone in the bright daylight and in the dark night.

God's eyes will see all living in the truth of His word and also those living in the devil's lies against this holy word that shines like the sun in the heart of every Christian who believes in God's Son, Jesus Christ.

He is the apple of God's eyes forever and ever, beyond the sun, moon and stars that will never disobey God who will never turn his eyes away from all who love and obey Him. He will not let you and me fall into the devil's traps if we keep our eyes on Him, who we will always see in His holy word.

God's all-seeing truth cannot lie to us about God, the Father, Son and Holy Ghost, who's all-seeing eyes are all over this world from coast to coast.

Eternity is All Present

Eternity is all-present, all around you and me as we live in this temporary world.

We will be temporary if our souls are lost under the bliss of the eternal heavens above mortal beings on earth.

We can abandon the eternal Son of God, rejecting Him and denying Jesus Christ in the land of the living surrounded by eternity, that is all present in God.

His eyes are all-seeing throughout eternity, beyond our temporary lives below the sky, where mortals can't beat God giving love that always lasts forever.

The grave is filled with bodies that rot away for the worms to eat way below the mountain cliffs.

Eternity hoovers in the love of an everlasting God.

He is eternal and eternity. He will give us immortality in return for loving Jesus with all our hearts.

He is all-present in eternity and will destroy the devil and his fallen angels with eternal death.

We can avoid this fate by choosing to follow the Lord and obeying Him beyond the visible temporary things that will one day pass away beneath eternity.

Then, we will be all present in the king of kings.

Shake Your Head at Me

O Lord, You have to shake your head at me for asking You to give me something that I don't need and looking like a fool because my prayer is selfish.

You will shake Your head at me for being unaware, and not knowing what I'm really asking You to do for me.

I can easily believe that I am selfless and always right about my prayer unto You, who are always selfless and right about what You say and do.

O Lord, You have to shake your head at me when I want You, Lord Jesus, to agree with me, who can be so wrong

I can be blunt about giving up on confessing and repenting unto you.

You shake your head at me, because I don't truly understand what I ask You to do for me.

You know what I can bear and not bear, but I don't know that and it shows in my prayers unto You.

Will Show Something

The Lord will show something to you that he will not show to me, and the Lord will show something to me so clear but He will not show it to you.

He knows that you are not me and I am not you.

To handle what God will show to you, search your own heart and be accountable.

Believe in his Son, Jesus Christ, because He will show all the world that he gave his life unto death to show us that we must deny self.

Jesus rose from the grave to show us that we can live in this world with a renewed life in Him.

He shows sinners great and small His love, and He wants to show us His mercy and grace.

You and I have a choice, whether to show or not show our faith in Jesus for anyone to see.

Our faith is something great to hold onto in this world.

Many people are living by what they see and things they have, which will surely fail them, rather than living through God.

Even though Jesus will show you something different from what I see, He means us both good and well under the sun.

Divine Moment

You and I can get caught up in a divine moment with the Lord, who's up in heaven above the highest mountain cliff beyond you and me.

God sends His holy spirit to inspire us with divine words and deeds, that make you and me on fire for the Lord.

He gives us divine moments through spiritual things that will never rust and erode.

We will get caught up in a divine moment unto the Lord for repenting of our sins.

We can get caught up in a bad moment of falling away from Jesus Christ, our Lord, on any day and any night.

God can make a moment divine for you and me, so we can shine our little light on time through the darkness in people's lives.

We are blessed in our divine moment of living right by God and it sets us free from lies. A bad moment passes away with no evidence it ever existed.

Jesus is coming back, so eternal and true.

His return is divine and we will get our rewards for obeying Him in this life.

Real

There are real people with real problems in the church.

You and I can go to church and be real with Jesus, who can work out any problem we have in our lives if we trust Him.

Jesus will not disappoint you and me, even when we just don't know what a powerful God we serve.

The Lord always knows who's real with Him in every way, beyond words to say so polished up and refined.

There are real people with real problems in the church of God.

God is never too far away up in heaven to hear our cries and feel our pain.

That pain is real to Jesus Christ, our Lord and our God.

Jesus became real flesh and blood on this earth, where he took our blame and sins and became the slain lamb of God.

God is so real for you and me, who have real problems every day that we can give to Jesus.

His true church is our hearts that can stray away from Him, if we don't love and obey Jesus so real every day.

There is No Love in Being Selfish

There is no love in being selfish, regardless of who we are under all the stars.

It's so easy to have a selfish heart and get too absorbed in me, myself and I.

You and I will always be below God in heaven on high.

He is above selfishness.

Love is being selfless and not using others to make ourselves look good.

Love is good all the time in selfless people, who aren't hooked on themselves.

You and I must deny selfishness and pick up our own cross and follow Jesus Christ.

He was selfless in every way that you and I can't ever imagine, especially when it comes to giving up His life on the cross for our sins so we may receive eternal life when he comes back, so selfless.

There is no love in being selfish, which will surely cause us to sin against God.

Our selfishness will never be a friend to anyone, no matter how we dress it up to look good climbing up the ladder of success.

We can never get above Jesus Christ.

He is love is all the time, in God in heaven above.

Selfish hearts are temporary and will one day pass away under the sun.

The Lord loves a selfless heart to pray to Him and obey Him every day.

The Lord's Green Light of Truth

We can drive through the Lord's green light of truth, which will set us free from living in darkness.

You and I can't live right in the church, if we drive through the Lord's red light of breaking his commandments of golden rules.

These rules are for all, great and small, who the Lord will not excuse from obeying Him.

We can know right from wrong by the Word that comes from God, who loves you and me with his long-suffering grace that's poured upon the whole world.

We have no excuse to not face up to His truth that has no red stop light for the Lord not to save our souls.

Going through hard times will be no excuse to drive through the Lord's red light of disobedience.

This will show and tell sooner or later in one's life.

We can drive through the Lord Jesus' green light of truth that has no lie to crash us into hell.

Anyone can go to hell for driving through God's red light of blaspheming his holy spirit, who speaks God's truth to our hearts.

We have no excuse to harden our hearts against God's green light of the truth, the way and the life in his Son, our Lord and Savior, who can make us right with God.

Below the Sky

Time is only below the sky, for time will one day run out.

There is no time beyond the sky being high above the ground that can shake and break apart from an earthquake.

Below the sky, hearts are only for God to know whether they are for Him or against Him day by day.

Death is below the sky because sin is way down in our nature, and we sin against God who is everywhere in heaven and on earth.

Only God cares to share his only Son with this fallen world below the sky.

Only sinners live and need to be governed by laws of God.

Only God's laws are holy and perfect to point out our sins to us here on earth.

Only human beings like you and me are created in the likeness of God, whose Son was born of the holy ghost in the womb of a virgin woman that God chose to represent his pure church.

The heart of time was right on time for Jesus.

The light of the world shines God's love to all the world below the sky.

Some who know me

Some who know me and believed that I would not prosper beyond my failures were so right, until my Lord proved them wrong.

After the Lord stepped in, none of their words were true about me.

I was doomed to be like the dirt on the ground being walked all over by their opinion of me, until Jesus Christ, my Lord, planted his seeds of mercy and grace down in the spiritual dirt of my soul.

I decided to make Jesus my bright sunshine and rain showers, and I decided to love and obey Jesus.

In the eyes of all who know me to have failed and be nothing in life, my bad choices made me look like a fool.

My Lord Jesus proved I was no fool, and He set me free from my failures.

Some who know me believed I'm not supposed to be blessed by the Lord.

The Lord will not deceive me, leave me or forsake me.

My trials are as high as a mountain, for my life too look so scared up in the eyes of who know me only by outward appearance.

My Lord Jesus brought me safely through it all, and now they are shocked.

Leaning to the Ways of Babylon

We church folks will lean to the ways of Babylon if we don't live the way we know to be right by God's holy word, which is for all to live by.

In these last days of the Babylon ways, it can deceive our eyes so we see no wrong in compromising God's word to fit in with the world's view of sin.

This world is no friend to Jesus Christ, the Son of God.

Jesus is calling you and me to come out of the spiritual Babylon making its way through the church and causing you and me to be no different from the sinful people of the world.

They lean to the ways of Babylon and come to church with no change of heart or willingness to do all that the Lord says to do.

These Babylonian last days people are leaning to their sinful ways that have led to spiritual adultery against God, who's ways are like a pure virgin with a loving heart.

Promise

My Lord Jesus, You never promised me that believing in you would be easy to do, especially in my dark days of disappointments and sorrow.

You, Lord Jesus, never promised me I'd live to see tomorrow.

I can only hope to see another day by living according to your will.

I can always trust You to be true to me, and I must deny my own will to follow you.

You, Lord Jesus, never promised me that it would be easy to follow you and work for you, but You always help me to love You and obey You by giving You all of my heart.

You, Lord Jesus, never promised me that it would be easy to march in your army and fight against an enemy I don't always see coming at me with his weapons of war to destroy me.

You, my Lord Jesus Christ, have promised me that you will never leave me or forsake me.

You fill me with Your holy spirit every time I ask You to give me the strength to live by Your word, which is a promise and spiritual meal.

You Were Always There for Me

My Lord, You were always there for me when I just didn't know.

You were there with me, way down in my low self that was being chewed up and swallowed down in the darkness of sin.

You, O Lord, found me in the utmost depths of my lost soul.

I didn't know how lost I was in the cold, chilly times of my life, but You, O Lord, were there for me.

I was too blind to see that you were there to set me free from the darkness of my unconfessed and unrepented sins.

You, Lord Jesus, stepped between death and me in my selfish lifestyle.

You bore the cross so I could receive a second chance to make You, O Lord, my all.

Knowing that You didn't give up on me meant everything.

I am still alive because of You, whose will is for me to do as if I've always been living right by Your word.

Jesus will not stop blessing you

Jesus will not stop blessing you, even if your spouse leaves you for no good reason.

Jesus will not stop blessing you, even if you get too sick to be able to work again.

Jesus will not stop blessing you, even if people leave your church.

People can't stop you from wanting to please Jesus.

If you love Jesus and keep His holy law, Jesus will bless you in the winter, spring, summer and fall.

If you were lying down on your death bed, Jesus would bless your soul and give you life again beyond the dead if you die being saved in Him.

Jesus will not stop blessing you for as long as you live your life loving and obeying Him.

He is the only one who can judge you, no matter who holds a grudge against you.

You can choose to never stop giving Jesus your heart, twenty-four hours around the clock.

Us All

The devil hates us all, whether we're a man, woman, boy or girl, and regardless of the color of our skin all around the world.

Jesus loves us all and will give us a mansion beyond the gates of pearls.

The devil hates us all, whether we're rich, middle class or poor.

Jesus Christ loves us all in these last days before He comes back again.

The devil hates us all, whether we're big or thin, on a diet or not on a diet.

Jesus Christ, our Lord God, loves us all and knows the true and false in our hearts.

The devil hates us all, whether we're straight, lesbian or gay.

Jesus loves us all and hates our sins, even to this day.

We must confess, repent and turn away from living in darkness so we can love God.

He gave us his only begotten son to save us from our sins that we will hate to live in if we love Jesus, our God.

Ways

You may not like some of my ways, and I may not like some of your ways.

Today, if we love Jesus, we will love one another so we can be saved for heaven above.

We all were born in sin that separates us in more than one way and causes us to have some dislikes that we don't always understand.

God hates sin but loves every sinner who repents and loves Him.

His ways are higher and always perfect beyond our ways that will be unpredictable, deceitful, selfish and sour if we don't give all of our ways to Jesus Christ.

Jesus is the way, the truth and the life, and he will sometimes work in mysterious ways.

All of His ways are holy and perfect above our flawed ways that the devil can deceive us with.

The devil can make us believe we can trust our own ways to always do us good.

Only the ways of Jesus are always selfless and will always do us good.

Pure and Innocent

Little children are pure and innocent, like a beautiful flower that blooms so pure and innocent in the hour of the early morning in the spring season.

A little child's prayer is pure and innocent to God, whose reasons are higher than the heavens.

God hears a child's prayer sounding so pure and innocent in His ears.

The heart of a child is so pure and innocent to God.

He always comes into his little children's' hearts.

Little children are pure and innocent, like the fresh air that we breathe in and out here and there and everywhere we go.

Little children are pure and innocent, like a little child who loves to pray to Jesus Christ and obey his golden rules.

I am Not Worthy

I am not worthy to speak Your holy name, O Lord.

You have no blemish and no blame upon Your holy name.

The holy angels love to sing about You forever and ever, which is still not long enough for You, O Lord.

I am not worthy to think upon Your holy name that will blot out my sins when I confess and repent unto You, my Lord and Savior Jesus Christ.

You will causee the demons to tremble more and more when I speak Your holy name.

You name has more power than weapons of war and death, twenty-four hours around the clock.

I am not worthy to say Your holy name from the tip of my tongue that will fade away without a trace before You, O Lord change your holy name in Your holy word that holy men written about You, O Lord.

You are my friend and stick closer to me than a brother.

I am not worthy to speak Your holy name that death could not defeat.

Your holy name can give peace and cause the storm to cease.

Jesus Christ was a Carpenter

Jesus Christ was a carpenter here on earth.

Whatever Jesus built must have been perfect here and there and everywhere.

What Jesus built must have amazed many other carpenters.

Didn't know that they were in the presence of the builder of the new Jerusalem holy city with twelve gates of pearls for you and me.

One day, we will walk through them wearing our white robes of righteousness.

Jesus was a carpenter of great love for all the world to be saved in God's wonderful grace that must have shined like the sun on Jesus' face that you and me will one day see if we build our trust in Jesus today.

We must sincerely make our calling sure in Jesus Christ, who must have been the greatest carpenter who ever lived on earth.

He is the builder of eternal things that never break down, rust or erode forever beyond the earth's crust.

Our Souls

Our souls are like a beautiful rainbow to the Lord, who glows His mercy and grace upon us.

Our souls are a beautiful, precious gemstone to the Lord.

He will fight our battles for us to win our prize of salvation to be saved below the sky.

Our souls are like a beautiful, precious pearl to the Lord.

His precious blood can wash us clean like we never sinned against Him, who gives us His green light to go and sin no more for our souls to be redeemed.

Fathers Who Love Their Children

Fathers who love their children are very good role models all around the world in every neighborhood.

Every girl needs her father's love, just like every boy needs his father's love.

Good fathers will give love and joy to their children.

Fathers who love their children will be in their children's lives and treat them real good.

Boys and girls can feel so empty on the inside if their fathers are not around to love them and guide them through life.

A father is supposed to do this for his children.

A father who loves Jesus Christ will not neglect his children and let them grow up in life without a father.

Every child needs a father to be good to them for the world to see.

The Lord, who is our heavenly Father, loves all of his children forevermore.

In Real Life

In real life, all the good guys will not win the good girls, and all the good girls will not win the good guys.

In this real world, a movie can't take the place of real life.

In real life, many people will hate one another rather than loving one another.

Love is always real to nurture and sustain life every day upon the land of the living.

No movie can take the place of real people living the real life.

Life is not an actor performing before you and me.

Jesus Christ, our Lord and Savior, created life to be real for us to live life believing in Him.

Only He can give us eternal life in, but we must do God's will in real life.

No movie can change this fact, no matter how good the movie is or how good it makes us feel from our heads to our toes.

Real life will always be real in us.

Movies are pretend and surely will not help us to be real with one another.

In real life, the Lord is forevermore real and offers us eternal life.

Will Give

A foundation will give its strong support under a very tall building.

We may not give strong support to all of our brothers and sisters in the Lord.

If we give a lot of our time to the TV screen, the TV will give us a lot of selfishness and no love.

Cell phones will give us their text message and unpredictable ringing that we may not give an honest answer.

We know that a green traffic light will change so honest to red and let us know to stop to avoid an accident on the road.

The rooftop will cover over the house, but many parents will not cover the rooftop of love over their children who need a lot of love.

The bed that we lay in will very often give us a good night's sleep.

We may not always want to give a deep thought to thinking on God's mercy and grace that bought us this far.

All that we do will tell our neighbors who we are.

All that we say will not give our neighbors enough proof for them to know that we are real about loving Jesus Christ.

The bible will always give us the whole truth, even when we may not always give Jesus our whole hearts or trust.

Jesus will give us salvation to be saved in Him, but sin will give us death to become nothing but dust.

God, Himself, Gave

God, Himself, gave the health message to Adam and Eve by telling them to eat the fruit from every tree except the tree of knowledge of good and evil.

Knowledge and evil existed in the midst of the garden.

Eve was the first creature on earth to reject God's health message.

This grieved the Holy Spirit as well as Adam.

The grieving Holy Spirit to dwelt in their bodies that God made perfect without sin in the beginning.

Adam and Eve had to leave the Garden of Eden, where they had it so good before they hardened their hearts against God and his health message that had no

Flaws.

All Adam and Eve had to do to stay in paradise was not eat the fruit forbidden by God.

He so loved Adam and Eve first to warn them.

Many people are eating from that evil tree today.

God could have struck Adam and Eve dead, but He was gracious and let them live despite their disobedience unto Him who will forget our sins if we confess and repent.

Why would we want God to bless our health if we eat what is bad for our health?

That makes the devil glad, just like what Adam and Eve did made God sad.

Ancient Women of Greatness

The mother of the human race and most beautiful woman who ever lived on earth from coast to coast and ocean to ocean was Eve.

This woman was beautiful, even in her old age.

She got pregnant and birthed a baby boy.

Sahar didn't believe that God was for real with her.

She laughed at God when he told her that she would conceive a child who would play a big part in His purpose to make a great nation.

A Levi woman gave birth to a second son, who grew up in the military art of the Egyptians.

Who was the first to practice the oppression of slavery, when God used the Levi woman's son to free the slaves to worship God who no one else except the Levi woman's son saw in a burning bush up on a mountain.

This woman was a prophetess and a wife who God inspired with a fountain of prophecies with new songs of victory over the Jabin king of Hazor ans Sisera, that Deborah prophesized to be defeated because of God's love for her and her Israelite people.

A very beautiful young virgin woman who entered into a beauty contest as she made a good impression and won the favor of Hegai who wasted no time to prepare Esther to win the contest to be crowned as the new Queen.

Esther became Queen through God's anointing upon her.

This young woman was a virgin and she was engaged to a man who loved her because she loved God like he loved God.

This man became distressed when he found out that his bride was pregnant, but he still loved her regardless of his doubts.

An angel appeared to Joseph in a dream and told Him that Mary was carrying God's son in her womb.

Can Carry

Mosquitoes can carry the West Nile disease that can spread for miles and miles and kill many people dead.

Rodents can carry the bubonic plague.

Many people can carry the AIDS Virus.

A poisonous snake will carry deadly venom in its fangs.

Many people will carry their heavy burdens all around the country, city, state and town, buzzing the sound of their complaints.

A man and woman can carry a load of romance for each other before they marry each other, to carry no load of responsibilities.

Knowledge can carry power.

Selfishness can carry greed and trouble twenty-four hours around the clock.

Love can carry a heavy weight of heartache.

Grudges can carry years and years of hate.

Life can carry us to age old.

Jesus Christ will carry our souls to heaven above, if we carry our hearts to obey God's commandments, that we will do, if Jesus is our first love.

We Know

We know that a house didn't build itself and we know that a boat didn't make itself float. We know that a car didn't build itself, and a car can't drive a itself anywhere near and far.

We know that an airplane didn't build itself, and we know that a train can't make itself run down a track.

We know that a shoe rack didn't build itself, and we know a bridge didn't build itself to be something we can cross.

We know that clothes didn't make themselves, and we know that a fountain didn't make the water in its basin.

We know that a mountain didn't build itself, and this world didn't create itself.

We know that a pearl didn't make itself, and we know that the universe didn't come about out of nothing.

We also know that God built the universe, the earth and everything upon it.

Are We Like

Are we like the beautiful green grass, growing so gracefully on God's holy ground where the wheat will outlast the tares?

Are we like the dried-up brown grass that won't grow spiritually on God's holy ground? We can know a lot of bible scriptures, but still scorch ourselves with pride.

Are we growing up like a tall tree on Gods holy ground where our spiritual growth can't hide?

Do we chop one another down with words on God's holy ground and then want the Lord to not chop us down like chopping down trees in the summertime when we need the shade to cool us off from the hot heat?

Are we like the leaves falling off the trees on God's holy ground?

Our ways can change colors like the leaves and fall down in selfishness.

God's word will never change on His holy ground in the winter, spring, summer and fall.

No one can blame the Lord Jesus Christ, if we fall down on the rebellious ground of sin.

Are we rooted in the truth to withstand the strong hurricane and tornado winds of false doctrines, strife and persecutions that won't uproot us for making Jesus our friend over this world?

Are we like bugs on God's holy ground where we can crawl judgmental words, trick words and high-minded words on all who insult our intelligence that God doesn't need?

Are we like beautiful flowers on God's holy ground, where our trust in Jesus will wither away if we claim to be self-powered to rule over the dark forces of evil that will tremble before Jesus every second, minute and hour?

The Righteousness of Jesus

The deep, deep waters have swallowed men of great stature and have made many men into waste on the bottom of the oceans, seas, rivers and lakes.

The mighty, strong winds have blown the breath out of many men.

The strong winds have calmed down with what God left behind, beyond the red-hot blazing fires that have burned up and neatly laid down the ashes of men on every land.

The dust of the earth has agreed with God to return men to dust, for men are better off dead than living forever in the sinful nature that is upon the flesh.

Men, even in the best of health, will get sick and die because sin can destroy.

The Lord Jesus Christ died for our sins and rose from the grave with the victory of eternal life.

He gave this gift to all men, women, boys and girls, who believe in Him.

He created all things in this world from nothing and He will surely bring the righteous dead back to life when He comes back again.

The righteousness of Jesus will never end.

In the School of Life

In the school of life, we will often learn things the hard way to discern a good lesson.

Life can teach us how not to put our trust in seen things that can do us a lot of spiritual harm and put our souls in danger of being lost.

In the school of life, experience is our best choice to make us wise up and not make the same mistakes over and over again in this very criticizing world.

We need to always be sober-minded in God's word and not get drunk in selfish desires.

The school of life can be no friend to bully us into living in sin against the Lord Jesus Christ.

He will cleanse us of our sins if we confess and repent for Him.

Jesus will give us a passing grade for us to see that God is for us.

The school of life can be against us whether we have or don't have a diploma or degree.

God's foolishness is wiser than men whose education is destructive if we don't use it for God's will.

It's a Very Thin Line

It's a very thin line between love and hate.

It can be hard to love our enemies and easy to hate them.

It's a very thin line between good and evil.

Doing good things can cause people to get jealous, and evil things can cause people to believe the green grass is really brown and the brown grass is green in their lives.

It's a very thin line between peace and strife.

It can be hard to make peace with anyone who's against you, and too easy to make strife between you and me.

It's a very thin line between the color of the skin.

I's so easy to accept anyone who looks like you and me and reject those who don't.

It's a very thin line between right and wrong.

It can be hard to do right, but so easy to do wrong for so long.

It's a very thin line between a wheat and a tare.

It's easy for a tare to look like wheat and wheat to look like tare in the church.

Only Jesus Christ can do the separating so easily.

It's so hard for us to not always know what's in our own hearts.

It's a very thin line between the dust of earth and the living flesh that was born in sin.

It's easy to die and lick the dust, and that's hard for us to forget.

We know that death has already taken many lives between the sunrise and sunset.

It's a thin line between what is yet to come to us.

We Must Love One Another

We must love one another to love God, who we don't see.

God created us all to love and be loved every day.

God loves us all, great and small.

We must love one another all the time in the fall, winter, spring and summertime.

If we don't love one another, we don't love God, whose love is so divine all the time beyond and below the sunshine.

God's love is always pure beyond our love that can be so ill to not cure a broken heart.

We must love one another so very real to love God who so loved us first, and send us his only begotten Son for all the other worlds in the universe to see that we are so loved by Him.

We must love God to be able to love one another.

If you and I don't love God, we don't love ourselves either.

We must love our creator God and everyone else.

Love is God, who gave us his Son from all of his heart.

We must love one another to love God and start our days off loving one another.

That won't be hard to do if we love God.

No One Can Question Jesus About Me

None of my enemies can question Jesus Christ about letting me live to see this day.

They can't question Jesus about why He gives me another day to live.

I can't question Jesus about death or when it will take me out of the blessings of life.

All of my loved ones can't question Jesus about my trials and troubles under the sun.

It will shine at the command of Jesus, to brighten up my day with the seasons of God's mercy and grace hovering over my soul.

The devil can't question Jesus and ask Him to let me die lost in my sins.

Jesus will give me a chance to choose to answer to Him in confession and repentance.

Jesus will question me about doing His will before it's too late.

No one can question Jesus about me at any time or day.

Jesus is not obligated to answer our questions.

We are not worthy to question Jesus' reasons about the good and bad things in our lives.

Jesus is the only one who can answer our questions in the heavens, if we are saved in Him.

No one can question Jesus about the answers He gave to our destiny when he rose from the grave.

If You Don't Love Jesus

You can be a hero, but if you don't love Jesus Christ you're living your life in vain.

You can be a legend in this life, but if you don't love Jesus your life is vain.

You can be famous, but if you don't love Jesus your name won't be in the book of life. You can be rich. but if you don't love Jesus your life is vain.

You can be popular but if you don't love Jesus our life is vain.

You can be a real patriot, but if you don't love Jesus you're living your life in vain.

You can be very beautiful, but if you don't love Jesus your life is vain.

You can be a genius, but if you don't love Jesus your life is vain.

You can be great, but if you don't love Jesus your life is in vain.

You can go to church, but if you don't love Jesus you're living your life in vain.

You can hold church positions, but if you don't love Jesus you're living your life in vain.

You can have spiritual gifts, but if you don't Jesus your life is vain.

You can be educated, but if you don't love Jesus you're living your life in vain.

If you don't love Jesus all that you say and do is vain in life.

Our choices

Our choices can make us wise.

Our choices can make us foolish.

Our choices can make us good.

Our choices can make us bad.

Our choices can make us prosper.

Our choices can make us poor.

Our choices can prolong our life.

Our choices can shorten our life.

Our choices can make us smart.

Our choices can make us stupid.

Our choices will make our destiny in heaven or hell.

We can choose to believe in Jesus Christ and be saved.

We can choose to live for the devil and be lost.

God gives us all free will to make choices.

The devil can't take our choices away from us.

Our choices will make us reap what we sow.

Our choices will make our character.

Our choices will make us moral or immoral.

We Are All No Good

We are all no good when it comes to Jesus Christ, who is so good to us all the time.

We can live a life of being good for selfish reasons.

Jesus' good is always selfless.

The words that we say can sound good, but may not be true.

Jesus' good is always true to everyone in every neighborhood.

The deeds that we do can be good, but we may want something good in return.

All that Jesus does is always true.

Jesus doesn't do good deeds for us just to get something good from us.

We wouldn't give Him our trust if he wasn't good to us.

We all are no good when it comes to Jesus, whose goodness leads us to repentance.

Our good can be from just going through the motions in a moment.

Jesus' good is all present in His holy law that is always good for us to keep in the fall, winter, spring and summer.

We are all no good when it comes to Jesus, who had lived on earth without sin.

We Will Forever Be Learning

We will forever be learning about Jesus Christ when we get to heaven to live out our eternal life.

We will forever be learning about other worlds in heaven when we get there living without sin.

We will forever be learning about the outer space and new galaxies to greatly embrace.

We will forever be learning about the holy angels and eating from the tree of life to hopefully have some mangos.

We will forever be learning about creatures in other worlds and get to know who they are.

I will forever be learning about you and you will be forever learning about me.

We will forever be learning about God, the Father, the Son and learning about the Holy Ghost, who's forever beyond all that we can learn.

We will forever be learning about all who will make it to heaven.

We will forever be learning about Jesus, who didn't fall into sin to save me and you.

In the Belly of the Whale

We are in the belly of the whale of injustice that swallows us down in not being treated right.

We are in the belly of the whale of right now, and we need Jesus Christ to bless us on his holy ground.

We are in the belly of the whale of time that swallows us down and leaves us not knowing when our time will run out.

We are in the belly of the whale of grief that swallows us down in sorrow from the loss of loved ones that have passed on.

We are in the belly of the whale of this world that will swallow us down into temporary things that have no love for us.

We are in the belly of the whale of non-believers in Jesus Christ, who forever existed before Jonah who sinned against God.

God put Jonah in the belly of the whale to show him that he must obey God.

We are in the belly of the whale of so many crimes being committed. They swallow us down and drown us in criminals the devil controls so they sin against God.

We are in the belly of the whale of a falling away from the church that many people are leaving for their own selfish reasons that hurts Jesus' heart.

Jesus is in the belly of the whale of every born-again believer in Him.

We will swallow Jesus down in our hearts until our lives end.

Feelings

A lot of people will get caught up in their feelings.

They believe that if it feels good it must be right.

Feelings can deceive you and me.

A woman can meet a man for the first time.

If he makes her feel good she may believe that he is right for her.

We can make the mistake of letting our feelings cloud our judgment in life.

We have a Lord and Savior Jesus Christ whose feelings didn't cloud his mind.

He kept His thoughts on His heavenly Father to help Him reason things through without sin.

A lot of people will let their feelings be their guide throughout the day, but what we feel may not be true.

We can't rely on our feelings to get us through life.

Feelings can get us into some trouble.

Many people have gotten into some trouble following their feelings, and it was lethal.

Jesus felt everything that we feel, but He didn't let his feelings cause Him to sin.

Bad feelings have caused many killings all around the world.

All good feelings are not true.

Many people will feel good about saying something wrong to me and you.

Many people will feel good about doing something wrong to me and you.

We can't always trust our feelings, but we can always trust Jesus.

Good Health

All the money in this world cannot buy good mental health and good physical health that is our greatest wealth.

If you have good mental health and good physical health you have everything, even if you are financially poor.

Jesus Christ, the King of Kings, was in perfect health in his mind and body.

He even healed many sick and demon possessed people.

You can be financially rich, but be poor in your health.

You and I can be financially poor, but be rich in health.

Good mental health and physical health is from the Lord, who can surely use well people to heal the land.

Jesus can use sick people, too, but if you are in good health, Jesus can use you so much more to win souls to Him.

Many sick people wish they were in good health, no matter where they live.

Good mental health and good physical health is worth more than all the money in the world.

Many rich and poor people don't understand what it means to take good care of your health.

Our Lord Jesus Christ loves to use us for being in good health.

The devil hates to see us in good health.

He knows that Jesus can't fully use us if we are not in the best of health.

Everybody in the Church

Everybody in the church is not hoping for me to be successful.

Even the body language of some church folks is not for you and me.

Everybody in the church is not for you and me to prosper in good mental health and physical health like we should for believing in Jesus Christ.

Everybody in the church will not be blessed by your ministry work and my ministry work because they believe we are not good enough to bless them and help them to draw closer and closer to Jesus.

Jesus gives everyone in the church a ministry work to bless others.

Everybody in the church will not address you and me like a brother or sister in the Lord.

They don't believe that you and I are good enough to be called a brother or sister .

They can't stop having bad opinions of you and me.

Everybody in the church and everybody outside the church belongs to Jesus, whose gracious hand can save everybody if they are willing.

Everybody in the church will not be saved.

Everybody in the church doesn't care about you and me being saved before it's too late.

Keep Your Eyes on Jesus

If you keep your eyes on political leaders, you will be lost in sin.

They are not perfect and without sin.

If you keep your eyes on entertainers, you will be lost in sin.

They are not perfect or without sin.

If you keep your eyes on athletes, you will be lost in sin.

They are not perfect or without sin.

If you keep your eyes on pastors, you will be lost in sin.

They are not without sin.

If you keep your eyes on elders, you will be lost in sin.

They are not perfect or without sin.

If you keep your eyes on church members, you will be lost in sin.

They are not perfect and without sin.

If you keep your eyes on me, you will be lost in sin.

I am not perfect or without sin.

If I keep my eyes on you, I will be lost in sin.

You are not perfect or without sin.

You and I can keep our eyes on Jesus Christ.

He is perfect and without sin.

Can Say

People can say good things about you, and people may say some bad things about you and give you a bad name.

People can say good things about you, especially in church, which seems to be filed with good people.

You can look so important in the church, but Jesus leaves no one out of having a closer walk with Him.

What is important is that what Jesus says about you.

He will represent you before God in heaven.

Jesus knows your heart, beyond your good words and good deeds that can be apart from your true motives and intentions.

Jesus sees everything so clear all the time.

People can speak very well of you, but only Jesus truly knows you.

People can say swell words about you, but they don't truly know you.

You and I can never fool Jesus.

We can fool ourselves and think we're so close to Jesus, until someone rubs you and me the wrong way.

Walking Through the Door of Life

Walking through the door of life can take us to some unexpected days that are not nice to us.

Walking through the door of life can disappoint us sometimes when we least expect it on the land.

Walking through the door of life can leave us with no clue about when we will grieve.

Walking through the door of life can take us from youth to old age, but we can't trust age to get us through the uncertain days.

Walking through the door of life will lead us to make choices day after day.

Walking through the door of life will open wide for us to meet the Lord.

Walking through the door of life can take us to exercise our faith in Jesus Christ, who is our abundant life that we can live doing God's will.

The door of life can shut its door on us, so real — life is short.

Only Jesus can keep the door open for us to walk to old age.

We Don't Know Life

We can know truth but we don't know what life can bring us today because it's so unpredictable.

We can know this world but we don't know life that is like a mystery that can't always be solved.

We can know what comes out of the heart but we don't know life that is like a wanderer looking for a star up in the sky to follow.

We can know what someone says but we don't know life, which can be like another language to make us confused.

We can know actions to be real, but we don't know life's actions that can fill this world with heartaches, disappointments and grief.

We can know what we believe, but we don't know life that Jesus Christ always knows for us to believe in Him in this life.

We can know that we will one day die, and we know that if we will live a lie without Jesus in our life, we will never be saved.

Chances

We take chances every day in some kind of way.

The Lord takes chances with us, even though we make the mistake of sinning against the Him.

When we lay down to sleep, we take a chance of not knowing that we will wake up.

When we leave our houses, we take a chance of not coming back to unlock the door.

The Lord takes chances with us whether we'll love Him and do His holy will that secures the chance that you I will take day after day.

Whatever we say, we take a chance that it will be effective.

Whatever we do, we take a chance that it will be effective in some kind of way.

The Lord takes chances with us to confess and repent of our sins to believe in Him who can save us from our sins.

Life is full of chances.

It's a slim chance to end up in heaven, when our hearts are selfish.

Jesus took the greatest chance to leave heaven and live among sinners to greatly advance in His saving grace.

Our chances are many through God's grace.

Doesn't Make You Better

Making a lot of money doesn't make you better than anyone who's making less money upon the land.

The Lord can give you wealth and He can take it away.

Being rich doesn't make you better than someone who's poor.

The Lord can take away your riches and leave you like you were never rich.

It's not good to boast about how much money you make.

The Holy Ghost has nothing to do with anyone who believes they are self-made.

It's never a good thing for you and me to put someone on a pedestal.

All good things come from the Lord, not from anyone else.

It's the Lord who opens doors, and He can shut them, too.

Having a lot of material things and being educated doesn't make you better than anyone who's less fortunate.

If you live by eyesight, you can bring deception to yourself.

It's only under the sun that sin exists to cause you and me to feel proud and be too be selfish in some kind of way.

Only Jesus Christ is worthy too be better than anyone.

You may talk loud and intelligently to get what you want, but you are no better than anyone in this life.

No Comparison

Our best dreams are no comparison to the new heaven and new earth that will have nothing to be called manmade.

The best technology is no comparison to the new heaven and new earth that will be filled with miraculous things for you and me to behold.

The most beautiful city on earth is no comparison to the new heaven and new earth that we will go to for being saved in Jesus Christ.

The most beautiful woman on earth is no comparison to the new heaven and new earth where we will have a perfect body and live forever with God who so loved us first.

The most brilliant minds are no comparison to the new heaven and new earth, where our minds will be perfect to understand all things.

The richest people on earth are no comparison to the new heaven and the new earth where wealth is eternal for you and me so we have riches forever and ever.

Religion here on earth is no comparison to the new heaven and new earth where we will be with Jesus Christ for being saved in Him.

Jesus will fill the new heaven and new earth with so many things that we cannot imagine.

Will Outweigh

Thanking You, O Lord, for all that you have done for me will outweigh what is not going right in my life that I see as my fault.

Thanking You, O Lord, for all that You are doing for me.

It will outweigh all the grief that is in my heart.

All the blessings that you give to me, O Lord, will outweigh the wrong things in my life.

Because of You, O Lord, I can shake off my disappointments and move on to a higher ground where You, my Lord Jesus Christ surely abound.

Being thankful unto You, O Lord, day after day will outweigh any obstacle that may come my way.

You, my Lord and Savior Jesus Christ, will always outweigh my life with the price that you paid for me to be saved in Your saving grace.

Growing Up in the Lord

There are people who grow up and do nothing much with their lives.

There are people who grow up and are out of touch with the real world.

There are people who grow up to be the best that they can be in life and greatly succeed.

Growing up in the Lord is the best way to grow up in this world, where spiritually mature adults see sin for what it is.

There are people who grow up and settle for less than the best.

There are people who grow up and make a mess of their lives.

Growing up in Jesus Christ is a life of doing God's holy will.

Growing up in Jesus is a growth of love for Jesus and our neighbors.

There are people who grow up and see no brighter day in their lives.

Growing up in Jesus is so full of brighter days, beyond the dark clouds of sorrow.

There are people who grow up to borrow nothing but trouble that they love to breathe in and out.

Growing up in the Lord Jesus Christ is a shout of joy to share with those who don't know Him but can choose to get to know Jesus and grow up spiritually, which is the best growing up to do.

Will Give Luck the Glory

Many people will give luck the glory that belongs to the Lord, who is merciful to spare lives through a bad accident.

Day after day, you and I can't put our trust in luck because bad things will happen according to the Lord allowing it to happen for His reason that is beyond our understanding.

Many people will give luck the glory that we should always give to Jesus Christ, who is so merciful to spare lives from a hurricane that brings in water to flood neighborhoods where many good citizens live.

Luck has no power to do what the Lord can do in His holy name.

Luck can't do anything for you and me, and luck can't save lives.

It's the Lord's mercy that save lives.

Many people will die from accidents and disasters that the Lord allows for His reasons, which many people will question and may not like the answer they receive.

It will be very lethal to our hearts to give luck the glory.

If we believe in luck to spare our lives, then we disown the Lord's mercy upon our lives.

Doing that leaves us bare-naked before the devil without the Lords mercy upon our souls.

Luck is the devil's work and causes many people to believe that the Lord has nothing to do with sparing lives from destruction that is so bold to kill us.

Give the Lord Jesus Christ the glory, not luck that is like a bad sore to the Lord.

Change

A lot of people live in the past.

They have a hard time with change.

Change is not a bad thing.

Many people are not worth a dime, and do not want to change for the better.

Change is nothing new under the sun, where Jesus Christ once lived without sin to change the world for the better.

Change began when Adam and Eve sinned against God, and then God couldn't let man live forever upon the land with sin.

There is change in every generation that is different in some kind of way.

Change is no friend to people who love to live in the past.

Jesus allows change to be known in a changing world where change has set many people free from oppression.

The Lord is for change, except when it comes to His holy word. That will never change and will always be a good thing for you and me.

Change is a bad thing to people who don't want to change for the better.

In every generation, many people have made a good name for themselves by accepting change that will always exist to the end of this world.

Love Can Surely Get Our Attention

Love can surely get our attention and allow us to enjoy being loved.

It can make us feel like a little child playing with our toys.

Love can surely get the attention of many criminals who don't understand what love is.

Love is the best cure for all upon the land.

There is nothing else like love to get our attention.

Love can surely get our attention more than any invention.

Love is like a whistle that we can blow loud to get people's attention when their minds may be up in the dark clouds of stress.

Wherever we go, love can surely get our attention.

Love is like a big hit movie that won't be a good movie without any love scenes in it.

Love can surely get our attention all day long.

People need to be loved; that is never wrong.

Don't make the mistake of believing that lust is love.

Love is surely from God in heaven above.

God's love is here to stay, when lust will come and go away.

We can't love without God, who is love every day to surely get our attention for giving us a free will.

Love can surely get our attention and can show us it's so real.

The Good You Put Off Today

The good you put off today maybe your last day to do something good for someone who may truly need your help.

The good you can do today, do in the name of the Lord who will do us good in many ways that you and I don't deserve.

You and I don't always see the Lord being so good to us.

The good you put off today may not happen tomorrow, because that is unknown for you and me.

We don't know what tomorrow may bring us.

You and I will borrow today from the Lord, who lends us today to live.

The good you put off today is like swallowing down a bad pill that can make you sicker to not do anything.

Tomorrow is not promised to us like someone who can't sing and believes that it sounds good.

The good you put off today when you can do it now, is like having a bad cold that's taking its slow time to go away.

We Don't Always Trust the Lord

We usually trust our ideas to be real.

The Lord is above our ideas.

We usually trust our reasons to be right.

The Lord is above our reasons all day and all night

We usually trust our opinions to be true.

The Lord is above our opinions, for he is the truth to set you and me free.

We usually trust our feelings.

The Lord is above all that we feel and brings us healing.

We don't always trust the Lord to protect us.

We usually put our trust in what we can do, but that can't always protect us.

We usually trust what we know.

The Lord is above all that we know.

He knows all things in heaven and on earth.

We don't always trust the King of Kings and the Lord of Lords to work out our problems that we often bring upon ourselves for not always putting our trust in the Lord.

The Lord's Tests

We don't always pass the Lord's test.

We don't see the test until the Lord shows it to us.

We can be so blind.

The Lord can allow danger to come our way.

He knows when we give Him less of our trust or more of our trust.

We all do fail some of the Lord's tests.

We can make it hard to pass, like not opening our mail to see if it's good.

The Lord's tests are always good to give us the strength that we need to hold onto Him who shows mercy on us when we fail.

He feeds our souls with His love.

The Lord can allow a disaster to test our faith in Him.

He will give us a passing grade for being like Job, who loved God so very real.

Job lost everything he had, even all of his children, but he didn't curse God.

The Lord's tests won't break our hearts, but will surely make our hearts spiritually strong and mature.

We don't always pass the Lord's tests.

He knows that we won't always pass all His tests in this sinful world below the heavens.

The Lord knows what we can handle and can't handle.

He won't test us more than what we can handle.

We can never test the Lord with our best test that makes no good sense to the Lord who is all-wise.

The Lord's tests are wiser than all of this world's intelligence that is so simple in his eyes.

God Created Man and Woman

A woman can't do everything that a man can do.

A man can't do everything that a woman can do.

A woman is not smarter than a man in every way.

A man is not smarter than a woman in every way.

A woman can do some things that a man can't do.

A man can do some things that a woman can't do.

A woman can do some things and get away with them, when a man can't.

A man can do some things and get away with them, when a woman can't.

God created man and woman to be different in some ways.

A woman can't feel everything that a man feels.

A man can't feel everything that a woman feels.

A woman can't see everything that a man can see.

A man can't see everything that a woman can see.

A woman can't reason everything that a man can reason.

A man can't reasons everything that a woman can reason.

God created man and woman to be different, but they can love each other very much.

God created man and woman in his likeness.

God created woman for man to love and not boss her around.

Will Always Look Out for Us

The Lord will always look out for us much better than we can look out for ourselves.

We don't always understand what we get ourselves into.

We don't always know what's ahead of us and can be so blank-minded about what could do us bad.

The Lord will always look out for all of his children who he loves so much each and every day.

We can't always look out for our good.

We don't always see what's coming our way that may be good or bad for us.

The Lord will always look out for us who can be so glad that He will look out for us even if we don't always believe that He will.

Jesus Christ, our Lord and Savior, looked out for our souls to be saved when he paid our price on the cross to truly fulfill His father's will.

Time will not always look out for us.

Time can come too late for us to have time to run from trouble.

Jesus will always look out for us if we put our trust in Him and not in time that can crush our dreams so they never come true.

Jesus will always look out for us if we love and obey Him.

We can have doubts about our dreams, but we should never doubt the Lord.

He will always look out for us, even when we least expect Him to open a door for us.

Jesus will always look out for us, even unto death, if we are saved in Him.

He will raise us up when He comes back, and give us eternal life beyond the grave.

Disguise

There are people who can disguise themselves and seem so nice, but they have evil in their hearts and might even take someone's life.

There are people who can disguise themselves and seem to be fun, but they have evil in their hearts and might want to kill someone with a gun.

There are people who can disguise themselves and seem to love you, but they have evil in their hearts and will chew you up with words and spit you out with hate.

There are people who can disguise themselves and seem so good, but they have evil in their hearts that can hurt your feelings.

There are people who can disguise themselves and seem so true to you, but they have evil in their hearts and will hurt you with a lie.

There are people who can disguise themselves and look like they're keeping God's holy law, but they have evil in their hearts to make someone look so small.

There are people who can disguise themselves and seem so righteous, but they have evil in their hearts to do wrong things to you and me.

There are people who can disguise themselves so seem like good Christians, but they have evil in their hearts and are hypocrites.

There are people who believe that they can fool everybody, as if no one can see them for who they are.

There are people who believe they can fool God by making excuses for their sins, but God always sees everyone and everything so clear.

Having Faith in Jesus

Having faith in Jesus is believing that he is the son of God.

Having faith in Jesus is believing that he is the light of the world.

Having faith in Jesus is believing that he can save us from our sins.

Having faith in Jesus is believing that he can make us right with God.

Keeping the commandments can't save us from our sins.

Keeping the commandments is showing our love for Jesus.

Having faith in Jesus is believing that he is the Savior of the world.

Having faith in Jesus will surely please God.

Having faith in Jesus is believing that he cannot fail us.

Having faith in Jesus is believing that we can give Him all of our trust.

Having faith in Jesus is having a personal relationship with Him.

Having faith in Jesus is believing that he is the bread of life.

Having faith in Jesus Christ is believing that he is the life eternal.

When Jesus comes back again

When Jesus comes back again, He will raise the righteous dead as if they never died below the heavens on high.

When Jesus comes back again, He will raise the righteous dead as if they never slept in the grave for thousands of years.

When Jesus comes back again, He will raise the righteous dead as if they never slept in the grave for hundreds of years.

When Jesus comes back again, He will raise the righteous dead as if they never slept in the grave for decades.

When Jesus comes back again, He will raise the righteous dead as if their bodies never rotted down to the bone.

When Jesus comes back again, He will raise the righteous dead with a immortal bodies.

When Jesus comes back again, He will raise the righteous dead with a perfect mind and body without sin.

When Jesus comes back again, He will raise the righteous dead to be taken up on the clouds of glory to go back to heaven with Him.

The righteous living will be changed to go with Jesus back to heaven.

Shouldn't Take for Granted

We shouldn't take our intelligence for granted, as if we were born to be intelligent. Intelligence is from the Lord.

We shouldn't take our talents for granted, as if we deserve to be talented.

Talents are from the Lord.

We shouldn't take our life for granted, as if we are worthy to live.

Life is from the Lord.

We shouldn't take time for granted, as if we have all the time in this world to be saved in Jesus.

Time is from Jesus Christ the Lord.

We shouldn't take one another for granted, as if its right to do that.

The Lord Jesus loves us all the same.

We shouldn't take this world for granted, as if our nation is better than other nations.

Jesus gave up his life to save souls in every nation.

We shouldn't take our health for granted, as if we can live forever in our body.

Our body belongs to Jesus, who loves to prolong our lives.

We shouldn't take Jesus Christ for granted, as if He is a fairy tale.

The bible tells us that Jesus is real, and to believe in Him is to be saved from our sins.

Give Jesus some of your time

Don't give all of your time to your job.

Give Jesus some of your time.

Jesus is the one who gives you the life, health and strength to work.

Don't give all of your time to getting an education.

Give Jesus some of your time.

No one can educate you better than Jesus.

Don't give all of your time to the TV.

Give Jesus some of your time.

Jesus wants you to pray and watch for Him to come back again on the clouds of glory.

Don't give all of your time to your dreams.

Give Jesus some of your time.

Jesus can make your dreams come true if it's in His will.

Don't give all of your time to this world.

Give Jesus some of your time.

This world will one day pass away.

All Jesus wants is some of our time.

Jesus knows that we need to do other things that He allows us to do.

Jesus is so fair and gives His time to all of us.

Can Only Do What God Allows

Technology can only do what God allows it to do.
Science can only do what God allows it to do.
Medicine can only do what God allows it to do.
Astronomy can only do what God allows it to do.
Evolution can only do what God allows it to do.
Time can only do what God allows it to do.
You can only do what God allows you to do.
I can only do what God allows me to do.
The devil can only do what God allows Him to do.
Natural disasters can only do what God allows it to do.
A nation can only do what God allows it to do.
The Government can only do what God allows it to do.
This world can only do what God allows it to do.
Man can't rise above God.
Woman can't' rise above God.
Nothing in this world can't' rise above God.
The devil can't' rise above God.
Angels can't' rise above God.
The universe can't' rise above God.
Heaven can't' rise above God.
God can do all things. Nobody can put a limit on God.

Doesn't Get People's Attention

Doing something good doesn't get people attention like doing something bad does.

Day after day and night after night, many people would rather hear about something bad than hear about something good.

We can be glad that Jesus Christ, our Lord, is all about doing something good for you and me and we should never doubt what Jesus can do for us. We can do a lot of good things that may not be acknowledged by the church congregation.

If we say something bad and do something bad in church, it will be known in the church so fast that you and I will fall down in the minds of judgmental church folks.

Doing something good doesn't get people's attention like doing something bad, and many people will use this to ruin a good name.

Doing something good doesn't always have a positive influence on people.

In This World

All the education in this world is like an inch on a yardstick compared to God's knowledge that will stretch eternal miles across outer space.

All the activities in this world are like a slow-moving turtle compared to one angel of God, who can fly faster than the speed of light.

All the beauty in this world is like dust on the shelf compared to a vision from God that is so true in beauty from heaven.

All the wisdom in this world is like dirt on the ground compared to the foolishness of God that is like streets made of gold.

All the bad things in this world are like a hole in the wall compared to God's anger that hell can't handle.

All the languages in this world are like one word compared to God's answer to our prayers.

All the motives and intentions that we have are like a clear crystal glass compared to God's reasons that we can't see or know why He allows some good people to die young.

All the living in this world is like a dream fading away in the bright morning sunlight compared to God's decision to let us live another day.

No One Will Ever

No one will ever do me right more than You, my Lord.

No one will ever help me more than You, my Lord.

No one will ever encourage me more than You, my Lord.

No one will ever motivate me more than You, my Lord.

No one will ever bless me more than You, my Lord.

No one will ever be true to me more than You, my Lord.

No one will ever tell me the truth more than You, my Lord.

No one will ever talk to me more than You, my Lord.

No one will ever look out for me more than You, my Lord.

No one will ever be close to me more than You, my Lord.

No one will ever touch my heart more than You, my Lord.

No one will ever know me more than You, my Lord.

No one will ever show me compassion more than You, my Lord.

No one will ever understand me more than You, my Lord.

No one will ever show me mercy more than You, my Lord.

No one will ever forgive me more than You, my Lord.

No one will ever love me more than You, my Lord and Savior Jesus Christ, who I need to love more than life.

www.ingramcontent.com/pod-product-compliance
Lightning Source LLC
Chambersburg PA
CBHW071303110526
44591CB00010B/754